Laura S. Brown brings together the best of the extant literature on feminist psychotherapy supervision and places it in the context of the broader scholarship on feminist therapy theory. This excellent, engaging book provides a model that is beneficial for feminist supervisors as well as for other psychotherapy supervisors who may wish to integrate insights and methodologies of feminist supervision into their work. Trainees would benefit from reading this book as well. Brown advances the belief that a feminist orientation increases the probability that all parties in the supervision triad—supervisor, therapist/trainee, and client—are transformed in a positive manner. This is an expanded purview of what constitutes feminist supervision and is thus a highly valuable contribution.

—Melba J. T. Vasquez, PhD, ABPP, Former President, American Psychological Association; Independent Practice, Austin, TX

In her newest work on feminist psychotherapy, *Supervision Essentials for the Feminist Psychotherapy Model of Supervision*, Dr. Laura S. Brown provides an invaluable resource for supervisors and therapists alike. The material is concise and clear, written in accessible language, and describes essential strategies and ways of relating across the supervisor-therapist-client triad. From one of the most senior and experienced supervisors in the field, the book promises to be a classic. It could not be more useful, and I'm sure every feminist supervisor, therapist, and student will want a copy.

—Ellyn Kaschak, PhD, Professor Emerita of Psychology, San Jose State University, San Jose, CA

An engaging, detailed, and well-organized deconstruction of feminist supervision which is also applicable to feminist leadership. The inclusion of a detailed history of feminism serves as a solid foundation for guidance in the provision of clinical supervision and consultation as well as leadership in organizations. This is a valuable must-read!

—Jessica Henderson Daniel, PhD, ABPP, Director, Psychology Training Program, Department of Psychiatry, Children's Hospital, Boston, MA

Supervision Essentials for

the Feminist Psychotherapy Model of Supervision

Clinical Supervision
Essentials Series

CLINICAL SUPERVISION ESSENTIALS

HANNA LEVENSON *and* ARPANA G. INMAN, Series Editors

Supervision Essentials for

the Feminist Psychotherapy Model of Supervision

Laura S. Brown

American Psychological Association • Washington, DC

Published by
American Psychological Association
750 First Street, NE
Washington, DC 20002
www.apa.org

To order
APA Order Department
P.O. Box 92984
Washington, DC 20090-2984
Tel: (800) 374-2721; Direct: (202) 336-5510
Fax: (202) 336-5502; TDD/TTY: (202) 336-6123
Online: www.apa.org/pubs/books
E-mail: order@apa.org

In the U.K., Europe, Africa, and the Middle East, copies may be ordered from
American Psychological Association
3 Henrietta Street
Covent Garden, London
WC2E 8LU England

Typeset in Minion by Circle Graphics, Inc., Columbia, MD

Printer: Maple Press, York, PA
Cover Designer: Mercury Publishing Services, Inc., Rockville, MD

The opinions and statements published are the responsibility of the authors, and such opinions and statements do not necessarily represent the policies of the American Psychological Association.

Library of Congress Cataloging-in-Publication Data

Names: Brown, Laura S., author.
Title: Supervision essentials for the feminist psychotherapy model of supervision / Laura S. Brown.
Description: Washington, DC : American Psychological Association, [2016] | Series: Clinical supervision essentials series | Includes bibliographical references and index.
Identifiers: LCCN 2015042276| ISBN 9781433822018 | ISBN 1433822016
Subjects: LCSH: Feminist therapy. | Psychotherapists—Supervision of.
Classification: LCC RC489.F45 B77 2016 | DDC 616.89/14—dc23
LC record available at http://lccn.loc.gov/2015042276

British Library Cataloguing-in-Publication Data
A CIP record is available from the British Library.

Printed in the United States of America
First Edition

http://dx.doi.org/10.1037/14878-000

Contents

CONTENTS

Foreword to the Clinical Supervision Essentials Series

We are both clinical supervisors. We teach courses on supervision of students who are in training to become therapists. We give workshops on supervision and consult with supervisors about their supervision practices. We write and do research on the topic. To say we eat and breathe supervision might be a little exaggerated, but only slightly. We are fully invested in the field and in helping supervisors provide the most informed and helpful guidance to those learning the profession. We also are committed to helping supervisees/consultees/trainees become better collaborators in the supervisory endeavor by understanding their responsibilities in the supervisory process.

What is supervision? Supervision is critical to the practice of therapy. As stated by Edward Watkins[1] in the *Handbook of Psychotherapy Supervision*, "Without the enterprise of psychotherapy supervision, . . . the practice of psychotherapy would become highly suspect and would or should cease to exist" (p. 603).

Supervision has been defined as

> an intervention provided by a more senior member of a profession to a more junior colleague or colleagues who typically (but not always) are members of that same profession. This relationship
>
> ■ is evaluative and hierarchical,
> ■ extends over time, and

[1] Watkins, C. E., Jr. (Ed.). (1997). *Handbook of psychotherapy supervision*. New York, NY: Wiley.

- has the simultaneous purposes of enhancing the professional functioning of the more junior person(s); monitoring the quality of professional
services offered to the clients that she, he, or they see; and serving as a
gatekeeper for the particular profession the supervisee seeks to enter.
(p. 9)[2]

It is now widely acknowledged in the literature that supervision is a
"distinct activity" in its own right.[3] One cannot assume that being an excellent therapist generalizes to being an outstanding supervisor. Nor can one
imagine that good supervisors can just be "instructed" in how to supervise
through purely academic, didactic means.

So how does one become a good supervisor?

Supervision is now recognized as a core competency domain for psychologists[4,5] and other mental health professionals. Guidelines have been
created to facilitate the provision of competent supervision across professional groups and internationally (e.g., American Psychological Association,[6] American Association of Marriage and Family Therapy,[7] British
Psychological Society,[8,9] Canadian Psychological Association[10]).

[2] Bernard, J. M., & Goodyear, R. K. (2014). *Fundamentals of clinical supervision* (5th ed.). Boston, MA: Pearson.

[3] Bernard, J. M., & Goodyear, R. K. (2014). *Fundamentals of clinical supervision* (5th ed.). Boston, MA: Pearson.

[4] Fouad, N., Grus, C. L., Hatcher, R. L., Kaslow, N. J., Hutchings, P. S., Madson, M. B., . . . Crossman, R. E. (2009). Competency benchmarks: A model for understanding and measuring competence in professional psychology across training levels. *Training and Education in Professional Psychology, 3*(4 Suppl.), S5–S26. http://dx.doi.org/10.1037/a0015832

[5] Kaslow, N. J., Rubin, N. J., Bebeau, M. J., Leigh, I. W., Lichtenberg, J. W., Nelson, P. D., . . . Smith, I. L. (2007). Guiding principles and recommendations for the assessment of competence. *Professional Psychology: Research and Practice, 38,* 441–51. http://dx.doi.org/10.1037/0735-7028.38.5.441

[6] American Psychological Association. (2014). *Guidelines for clinical supervision in health service psychology.* Retrieved from http://www.apa.org/about/policy/guidelines-supervision.pdf

[7] American Association of Marriage and Family Therapy. (2007). *AAMFT approved supervisor designation standards and responsibilities handbook.* Retrieved from http://www.aamft.org/imis15/Documents/Approved_Supervisor_handbook.pdf

[8] British Psychological Society. (2003). *Policy guidelines on supervision in the practice of clinical psychology.* Retrieved from http://www.conatus.co.uk/assets/uploaded/downloads/policy_and_guidelines_on_supervision.pdf

[9] British Psychological Society. (2010). *Professional supervision: Guidelines for practice for educational psychologists.* Retrieved from http://www.ucl.ac.uk/educational-psychology/resources/DECP%20Supervision%20report%20Nov%202010.pdf

[10] Canadian Psychological Association. (2009). *Ethical guidelines for supervision in psychology: Teaching, research, practice and administration.* Retrieved from http://www.cpa.ca/docs/File/Ethics/EthicalGuidelinesSupervisionPsychologyMar2012.pdf

The *Guidelines for Clinical Supervision in Health Service Psychology*[11] are built on several assumptions, specifically that supervision

- requires formal education and training;
- prioritizes the care of the client/patient and the protection of the public;
- focuses on the acquisition of competence by and the professional development of the supervisee;
- requires supervisor competence in the foundational and functional competency domains being supervised;
- is anchored in the current evidence base related to supervision and the competencies being supervised;
- occurs within a respectful and collaborative supervisory relationship that includes facilitative and evaluative components and is established, maintained, and repaired as necessary;
- entails responsibilities on the part of the supervisor and supervisee;
- intentionally infuses and integrates the dimensions of diversity in all aspects of professional practice;
- is influenced by both professional and personal factors, including values, attitudes, beliefs, and interpersonal biases;
- is conducted in adherence to ethical and legal standards;
- uses a developmental and strength-based approach;
- requires reflective practice and self-assessment by the supervisor and supervisee;
- incorporates bidirectional feedback between the supervisor and supervisee;
- includes evaluation of the acquisition of expected competencies by the supervisee;
- serves a gatekeeping function for the profession; and
- is distinct from consultation, personal psychotherapy, and mentoring.

The importance of supervision can be attested to by the increase in state laws and regulations that certify supervisors and the required multiple supervisory practica and internships that graduate students in all professional programs must complete. Furthermore, research has

---

[11] American Psychological Association. (2014). *Guidelines for clinical supervision in health service psychology.* Retrieved from http://www.apa.org/about/policy/guidelines-supervision.pdf

confirmed[12] the high prevalence of supervisory responsibilities among practitioners—specifically that between 85% and 90% of all therapists eventually become clinical supervisors within the first 15 years of practice.

So now we see the critical importance of good supervision and its high prevalence. We also have guidelines for its competent practice and an impressive list of objectives. But is this enough to become a good supervisor? Not quite. One of the best ways to learn is from highly regarded supervisors—the experts in the field—those who have the procedural knowledge[13] to know what to do, when, and why.

Which leads us to our motivation for creating this series. As we looked around for materials that would help us supervise, teach, and research clinical supervision, we were struck by the lack of a coordinated effort to present the essential models of supervision in both a didactic and experiential form through the lens of expert supervisors. What seemed to be needed was a forum where the experts in the field—those with the knowledge *and* the practice—present the basics of their approaches in a readable, accessible, concise fashion and demonstrate what they do in a real supervisory session. The need, in essence, was for a showcase of best practices.

This series, then, is an attempt to do just that. We considered the major approaches to supervisory practice—those that are based on theoretical orientation and those that are metatheoretical. We surveyed psychologists, teachers, clinical supervisors, and researchers domestically and internationally working in the area of supervision. We asked them to identify specific models to include and who they would consider to be experts in this area. We also asked this community of colleagues to identify key issues that typically need to be addressed in supervision sessions. Through this consensus building, we came up with a dream team of 11 supervision experts who not only have developed a working model of supervision but also have been in the trenches as clinical supervisors for years.

---

[12] Rønnestad, M. H., Orlinsky, D. E., Parks, B. K., & Davis, J. D. (1997). Supervisors of psychotherapy: Mapping experience level and supervisory confidence. *European Psychologist, 2,* 191–201.

[13] Schön, D. A. (1987). *Educating the reflective practitioner: Toward a new design for teaching and learning in the professions.* San Francisco, CA: Jossey-Bass.

We asked each expert to write a concise book elucidating her or his approach to supervision. This included highlighting the essential dimensions/key principles, methods/techniques, and structure/process involved, the research evidence for the model, and how common supervisory issues are handled. Furthermore, we asked each author to elucidate the supervisory process by devoting a chapter describing a supervisory session in detail, including transcripts of real sessions, so that the readers could see how the model comes to life in the reality of the supervisory encounter.

In addition to these books, each expert filmed an actual supervisory session with a supervisee so that her or his approach could be demonstrated in practice. APA Books has produced these videos as a series and they are available as DVDs (http://www.apa.org/pubs/videos). Each of these books and videos can be used together or independently, as part of the series or alone, for the reader aspiring to learn how to supervise, for supervisors wishing to deepen their knowledge, for trainees wanting to be better supervisees, for teachers of courses on supervision, and for researchers investigating this pedagogical process.

ABOUT THIS BOOK

In this book, *Supervision Essentials for the Feminist Psychotherapy Model of Supervision*, Laura S. Brown takes the qualities predictive of good supervision across models (e.g., openness, authenticity, self-examination, self-disclosure) and expands them to another level by considering the larger sociopolitical context in which clients, therapists, and supervisors function. From this feminist/multicultural position, supervisors focus on promoting supervisees' autonomy and diverse perspectives. They view their responsibilities as including advocacy roles on behalf of supervisees in the training setting and clients in the clinical setting.

Dr. Brown provides many compelling case studies to help the supervisor understand how to wrestle with creating a model of psychological practice that is, in her words, "liberatory as well as healing." With each chapter, she demonstrates how supervision is conducted to not only analyze power dynamics but also actually strive to *be* a social justice practice. No matter what your orientation (politically, socially, or clinically), Dr. Brown's approach is enormously powerful to help us consider the responsibilities of what it means to be a clinical supervisor and bring a contextual, collaborative, and interpersonal focus to the supervisory process.

We thank you for your interest and hope the books in this series enhance your work in a stimulating and relevant way.

Hanna Levenson and Arpana G. Inman

Preface

I am a practicing feminist therapist. With the exception of 8 years spent in academia, 3 at the beginning of my career and 5 in the early part of this century during which I maintained a part-time practice, I have been in full-time practice as a feminist therapist since I received my doctorate in 1977. I have been practicing supervision in both academic and private-practice settings since 1 month after receiving that degree. Like many supervisors of my cohort, I received no formal training in supervision. Instead, my having a doctorate and a faculty position was treated as evidence of my ability to supervise.

My own formal supervision experiences during my doctoral training before internship can be described as ranging from dismal to appalling. Few of the people who formally supervised me in my graduate program had seen a client after their own internships, all of which had occurred many years before I started graduate school. Consistent with their age cohort, none of them had thought about dynamics of gender and power in psychotherapy or their own lives, and they were ill-prepared to encounter an angry, well-read, and energetic young feminist student confronting them about sexism at every turn. Some of them were uncomfortable with my being the first open lesbian of their acquaintance, and what is now described as aversive bias (e.g., nonconscious bias that is at odds with people's conscious values of being unbiased) often leaked into our interactions.

Hired into my first academic job as I fell out of graduate student status and into that of faculty at my doctoral program, I was immediately given the task of running a feminist therapy supervision practicum, something that I had been among those clamoring for while I was still a student. I had no formal course work in supervision and several less-than-outstanding supervisory experiences. It seemed that, just as feminist therapy was then about not doing what was generally being done by therapists, feminist supervision would be an attempt to remediate the problems that I had experienced while infusing my understanding of what feminist therapy meant into the supervisory process.

This was a trial by fire for me and everyone in the group, as we tried to juggle role overlap (almost everyone I was supervising in the group that year was a friend and former peer from my doctoral program or a friend and colleague from the feminist community in our small university town), power dynamics (although I was the faculty member, I was years younger and sometimes decades younger than the people I was supervising, which created interesting and challenging explorations of power and privilege), my growing awareness of what it meant to have legal and ethical responsibility for the work of others (and my post-hoc appraisal of my great fortune in supervising a collection of ethical, thoughtful people), and the thorny question of evaluation (somewhat evaded by the pass–fail nature of the course, but never entirely out of mind, especially when I had second thoughts about what people were doing with their clients). It was my introduction to being in a defined position of power, which in turn taught me new and enlightening ways to consider and understand power dynamics.

I stumbled and fell quite a lot that year; I was fortunate in that the collective that was the supervision group contained many mature feminists, many of them from among my peer consultants, who shared the goal of discovering what feminist supervision could mean and who supported my professional development as an infant supervisor every bit as much, and perhaps more, than I was able yet to support their growing capacities as feminist therapists. It was a study in the reciprocity and mutuality that came to be identified as core to feminist supervision. I emerged from that year knowing how much I liked supervision and how much I needed to learn to do it well. In my next, also brief, academic position, I sought out opportunities to supervise, encountering many of the same conundrums that had challenged me in my first job (e.g., power issues arising from my junior age juxtaposed with my academic position relative to the doctoral students I was training), and becoming increasingly aware of the importance of supervision for imparting feminist principles to trainees who were not, in contrast to my first supervision group, already familiar with and grounded in feminist constructs.

When I left my paid position in academia in 1980 for full-time private practice, I retained an appointment as an adjunct faculty for the simple goal of being able to continue to supervise doctoral students. I had been bitten by the bug. Over time, as I published in the field of feminist therapy theory and practice, I also began to be increasingly sought out as a consultant by other psychotherapists. During the 1980s and 1990s, feminist therapy educators, chief among them Natalie Porter, began to write about feminist supervision. Reading this material has constituted my formal education on this topic.

The reality is that like many psychologists of my cohort of psychotherapy supervisors, I have learned by doing, attending to what was and was not helpful to me, and what I learned, from those I supervised, was and was not helpful to them. In 2006, on the heels of leaving a second brief stint in academia, I founded a feminist therapy training clinic, the Fremont Community Therapy Project, where, between 2006 and 2015, I was able to directly supervise many pre- and postdoctoral trainees every year. Those 60 women and men have, in turn, taught me infinitely more about how feminist therapy theory applies to the practice of supervision. They have given me unasked-for opportunities for difficult supervisory encounters that have honed my skills and challenged my understanding of how to apply principles of egalitarianism in the context of a necessarily hierarchical supervisory relationship. They have taught me how to remediate a problematic trainee from a feminist perspective and schooled me in the limitations of an empowerment model. They have been a lens and a mirror in which I have been required to observe myself and my struggles with applying egalitarian principles to supervision practice; without them, I could never have considered embarking on the project of this book.

It is solely because of the people I have supervised that anyone today considers me an expert supervisor worthy of writing this book. As has been true for me as a feminist therapist, whose best teachers have been my clients, so also for me as a feminist supervisor, whose best teachers continue to be the people I supervise.

Acknowledgments

Thanks are due to trainees, friends, and colleagues whose work contributed to my ability to conceptualize this topic. Natalie Porter, PhD, has been the guiding light to everyone in the field of feminist psychotherapy supervision. Without her work and both her initial and continuing theoretical frameworks I would not have known how to venture into this topic. Her wise counsel continues to inform me as a supervisor.

Dana Waters, PsyD, ABPP, served as a collegial research assistant, kindly making available to me through her own academic library access several references to which I would not have otherwise been able to easily gain access. Her willingness to do so has allowed me to engage in a more thorough and complete review of the literature on feminist supervision and thus to make this volume fully aligned with the work being written by others in the field. Dana has also been a tireless volunteer supervisor at the Fremont Community Therapy Project (FCTP), thus contributing directly to the feminist context in which I have been able to develop this supervision model.

Samantha Slaughter, PsyD, my not-so-junior-any-longer colleague, has been an invaluable companion as I developed my work as a feminist supervisor. Our cosupervision of trainees at the FCTP between 2009 and 2014 was an eye-opening experience that taught me yet another strategy for creating egalitarian and empowering supervision relationships. Samantha also did me the honor of being the supervised person in

Feminist Therapy Supervision, the companion DVD that is discussed in this book; her participation energized and inspired me to do my best work.

Finally, every person whom I have supervised since 1977 has taught me how to be a feminist supervisor and has given me the experiential knowledge that is foundational to my model of feminist supervision. I wish to especially thank the women in the first feminist therapy practicum at Southern Illinois University in 1977–1978, and the 60–plus people who were trainees at the FCTP between 2006 and 2015. Special thanks to Lena Swanson, PsyD; Carolyn Coyle Matthews, PsyD; Sierra Swing-Kent, PsyD; and Melanie Mitchell, PsyD, who collectively had the idea that I should start a training clinic for their practicum experience (Lena and Carolyn) and start an internship track in said clinic (Sierra and Melanie). You all pushed me over the edge of "can I do this" to "collectively, as feminists, we can make this work somehow." Which we did. Without the experience of running FCTP for the past decade, I would know so much less about feminist supervision.

The case examples in this book represent an amalgam, in each instance, of two or more individuals, whether the people being described are trainees or their clients. Every effort has been made to disguise details of the parties who inspired those examples. Specific details about myself and the supervision video that accompanies this book are not disguised and are included with the knowledge and active participation of Dr. Slaughter.

And as is always the case, I am eternally grateful to my clients, who have taught me the most important things I know about being a therapist and who continue to inspire me to excellence in all of my professional endeavors.

Supervision Essentials for

the Feminist Psychotherapy Model of Supervision

Introduction

Compared with the now-voluminous literature on feminist psychotherapy, relatively little has been written about supervision and consultation from a specifically feminist standpoint. Although literature on feminist therapy practice began to be published in the early 1970s, the first scholarly work on the topic of supervision in feminist therapy was not published until well into feminist therapy's second decade (Porter, 1985). In the intervening 30 years, there has been only a small amount of formal scholarship or research on feminist supervision.

There has been slightly more research on the related topic of gender in supervision, with a tendency to focus on women as supervisors and supervisees (Worell & Remer, 2003), and on modalities for incorporating feminist and multicultural perspectives into the supervision process (Miville, 2013). Much of the work done since Porter's original publication has expanded upon and echoed the themes she initially identified. More recent work

http://dx.doi.org/10.1037/14878-001
Supervision Essentials for the Feminist Psychotherapy Model of Supervision, by L. S. Brown

includes discussions of multicultural issues and of men as feminist therapists, reflecting the transformations in feminist therapy theory in the intervening three decades. But the literature on all related topics is sparse, and the
construct of feminist supervision has not been fleshed out in great detail.

This paucity of literature does not reflect the realities of feminist practice. According to anecdotal evidence from decades of interaction with
colleagues, many feminist therapists practice supervision, both in formal
training settings, such as practicum and internship sites, and informally in
private supervision and consultation practices. This book is long overdue.

This book attempts to bring together the wisdom of the extant literature on feminist perspectives in psychotherapy supervision, placing it in
the context of the more extensive scholarship on feminist therapy theory,
and exploring the supervisory practices most likely to emerge from the
application of feminist therapy theory to the supervisory context. This
book aims to assist supervisors who are feminist practitioners and feminist
practitioners who are interested in the practice of supervision to have a
more clearly delineated framework for the translation of feminist therapy
constructs into the supervision setting. In addition, this volume attempts
to demonstrate ways in which feminist therapy supervisory norms com-
plement, contrast with, and challenge norms of other supervisory models.
Finally, this volume invites psychotherapy supervisors who do not have
a feminist perspective to consider how they might integrate some of the
insights and methodologies of feminist supervision into their work.

FEMINIST ANALYSIS AND SUPERVISION

A hallmark of all good psychotherapy supervision is that all parties in
the triad—therapist/trainee, client, and supervisor—are transformed in
a positive manner by the supervisory experience. This volume advances
the argument that the feminist emphases on analysis of power, the disruption of oppressive narratives that emerge in the psychotherapy process
via an integrated analysis of experiences of oppression and dominance
(Kanuha, 1990), and development of systemic methodologies for generating egalitarian relationships in therapy and supervision all function
to increase the probability of positive psychotherapy outcomes. Feminist

psychology's attention to understanding and interrogating the experience of living a gendered life is an additional dimension differentiating feminist supervision from other approaches. Although gender may be addressed by other supervisors, it holds a central place in feminist analysis.

Feminist supervisory models are among those, including multicultural and critical psychology supervisory models (Miville, 2013), that explicitly identify the toxic effects of pervasive bias on the supervisory and psychotherapy processes. By its nature, feminist supervision embodies a commitment to the interrogation and disruption of manifest and non-conscious biased modes of relating, with an emphasis on the manner in which bias about gender and other aspects of identity affect relationship and psychotherapeutic dynamics. Feminist supervision has a sharpened focus on those dynamics in the therapist–supervisor–client relationship, particularly in the many instances in which any member of the supervision triad is devalued or disempowered by systemic aspects of social hierarchy. Feminist practices engage with and challenge assumptions about pathology or incompetence of the persons with lesser role power in those relationships. Feminist analysis is particularly attentive to the assumptions about normalcy and pathology that arise from biases and stereotypes about gender. Feminist supervision thus situates itself within the larger framework of feminist pedagogy in psychology (Enns & Forrest, 2005; Enns & Sinacore, 2005) as a liberatory project in which supervisor and supervisee join together to think critically about dominant cultural norms in the practice of psychotherapy.

The task of the feminist supervisor is not simply to train students in the practice of psychotherapy or the application of particular evidence-based interventions. Instead, the goal of a feminist supervision practice is to invite trainees to see how that practice upholds or subverts oppressive gendered norms in psychotherapy practice and in the larger social context. Similar to the goals of feminist psychotherapy, the feminist supervision model locates pathologies and failures of competence not in vulnerable individuals but in the rigidities and biases of the larger systems in which they struggle to exist.

Feminist therapy supervision is inherently developmental and strength based. It consequently attends to where both supervisor and supervisee are in their professional and personal identity developments and is tailored to meet the specific needs of the individual supervisee while assuming that she or he will progress developmentally in the course of the supervisory relationship. (This process of professional development is exemplified by the supervision session depicted in this volume's companion DVD, *Feminist Therapy Supervision*, which is discussed in detail in Chapter 3. The session represents the 13th year of a supervisory relationship between the two parties.) Feminist supervision practice acknowledges strengths and skills brought to the experience by both parties, not simply those of the supervisor. The concept of *covision* (Porter & Vasquez, 1997), to be discussed in detail later, assumes a reciprocity and forms of mutuality occurring between feminist supervisors and supervisees. The power dynamics that are inherent in supervision relationships in formal training settings are not ignored, but the feminist supervisor is directly curious about how power can become more equalized as supervision progresses.

SUPERVISION OR CONSULTATION?

In this book I refer to supervision and consultation practices as supervision because both involve in vivo education in psychotherapy practice through various combinations of didactic information about treatment, exploration of the person of the therapist, and learning through modeling and discussion about applications of theories and models of intervention. However, these two functions occur within two different legal frameworks, which in turn affect the power dynamics in the relationship. Clarification of which kind of relationship is occurring is a first step in feminist supervision/consultation. Throughout this book, supervision and consultation are addressed as one, except for instances in which the dynamics created by evaluation, gatekeeping, and screening for impairment differentiate the applications of feminist principles to the specific sort of practice.

Supervision is defined as occurring in an educative context in which the supervisor has legal and ethical responsibility for the practice of the person being supervised; in this context, issues of evaluation and gatekeeping are omnipresent. Participation in supervision is required for the trainee to achieve educational or licensure goals, and successful completion of supervised work is mandatory, not optional. In supervision, the supervisor's power is accentuated by these contextual and systemic variables.

Consultation is defined as occurring when a practitioner who is already fully licensed for practice voluntarily seeks supervisory support from a colleague who is neither ethically nor legally responsible for the consultee's practice. Participation in consultation is optional and voluntary, and there are no formal penalties for withdrawing from the consultative relationship. In a consultation relationship, issues of evaluation and gatekeeping are less salient and a more clearly egalitarian model of interaction is possible. However, even in the context of consultation practice, concerns regarding practitioner impairment may arise, particularly in a jurisdiction in which mandatory report of impairment in health care practitioners is present. In addition, there are subtle factors having to do with reputation and client referral that can add to the power of the consultant even though she or he does not have the same power as a supervisor. The case example discussed in Chapter 3, deriving from this volume's companion DVD, is a consultation session with a junior colleague in which the relationship initially was one of formal supervision.

Each of these situations creates hierarchies of power that are distinctive and to some degree required by the legal frameworks surrounding the relationship. These hierarchies generate challenges for the effective application of feminist models of empowering and egalitarian relationships. For feminist practitioners, this amount of role power and control with clear consequences for noncompliance by the recipient of services generally is not a component of psychotherapy practice outside of work in prisons (Cole, Sarlund-Heinrich, & Brown, 2007; Quina & Brown, 2007). The feminist therapist considering offering supervision services must adapt her or his strategies for empowerment and the development of egalitarian relationship to those legal and ethical requirements.

WHO SHOULD READ THIS BOOK?

The intended audience for this book is diverse and includes practicing supervisors of any theoretical orientation who are interested in deepening their capacities to understand the dynamics of gender and power as they influence the psychotherapy process. Because many psychotherapy supervisors today trained in a time when they were offered little or no exposure to feminist therapy theory and practice, they may be unaware of the degree to which feminist principles integrate well into most other models of psychotherapy or the many ways in which feminist constructs have become accepted as standards for good practice with their feminist roots often obscured. Having a clear notion of the paradigm informing an empowerment, egalitarian, collaborative model of practice can improve one's applications of that model. Feminist therapy theory is inherently integrative because it is concept driven, not intervention focused; thus, a feminist model of supervision lends itself well to integration into other supervisory models.

A second intended audience for this book is feminist therapists who have been practicing supervision without a clear model for how to implement feminist therapy principles into supervisory work. Because the literature on feminist therapy supervision is sparse and scattered across many different volumes and professional journals, it can be difficult for feminist therapists to familiarize themselves as completely as they would wish with the depth and breadth of what exists. It can also be daunting to uncover the pathways by which thinking about supervision has evolved in the field of feminist therapy during the past three decades. This book offers a convenient synthesis of the literature and encapsulates where the field stands in the early 21st century.

Finally, and perhaps most important, this book is for trainees in psychology and other psychotherapy professions. This book is for you for two reasons. First, I hope to give you an idea of what is reasonable to expect from a feminist therapy supervisor; I want to help you raise the bar for yourself and your supervisors so that the quality of your supervisory experiences can become more empowering and positive. Second, you are the supervisors of the future. Some of the best work and almost all of the research in the field of feminist therapy supervision is being written by graduate students and early career professionals whose grounding in feminist, multicultural, and liberatory models of psychotherapy has occurred from the beginning of their careers.

OVERVIEW OF THIS BOOK

In Chapter 1, I review the basic principles of feminist therapy theory. Research on feminist supervision has demonstrated that adherence to feminist values coupled with familiarity with the norms of feminist therapy is the best predictor of whether a supervisor is able to practice feminist supervision. Much of Chapter 1 reprises my earlier volume on feminist therapy (Brown, 2010), which is suggested reading for readers who are less familiar with the specifics of this orientation to practice.

Chapter 2 explores what I consider to be the essential dimensions and methodologies of feminist supervision practice. The chapter analyzes and synthesizes the work of many other theorists in feminist supervision, chiefly that of Natalie Porter and her colleagues. It explores specific issues that a feminist supervisor should strive to address in work with trainees.

Chapter 3 builds on this book's companion DVD, *Feminist Therapy Supervision*, using the work done on camera by Dr. Samantha Slaughter and me in a supervision session. The chapter introduces themes of common processes in feminist therapy supervision, illustrating it with specific examples from the companion DVD. The DVD and chapter address how a feminist supervisor actively practices the constructs of feminist supervision.

Chapter 4 explores some of the common challenges inherent in applying feminist principles to supervision and consultation. Using case examples drawn from my experiences as well as those of other experienced feminist supervisors, I illustrate how the feminist model of empowerment and egalitarian relationships with trainees lend themselves well, and are challenged by, supervisees who are struggling in a variety of ways with the learning process. The chapter also offers some ideas about how remediation for trainees who are struggling with skill and personal development can be generated within the feminist framework.

Chapter 5 reviews the still-sparse literature on feminist supervision. It draws on the findings of that literature to develop suggestions for research and discusses possible future directions for feminist supervision practice.

The book concludes with a brief list of suggested readings on the topic of feminist therapy supervision. The readings attempt to capture the conceptual roots of the field and current thinking.

Finally, in Appendixes A through C, the book includes several administrative forms that may be of practical use for supervisors. The Feminist Therapy Institute's Code of Ethics is also available for reference in Appendix D. These documents can also be downloaded from the American Psychological Association website (http://pubs.apa.org/books/supp/brown).

CONCLUSION

Feminist therapy supervision strongly reflects practices in feminist, multicultural, queer, and other critical psychologies. As such, it challenges all participants to attend to assumptions about the presence or absence of bias and the ways in which power distributes itself, both formally and informally, in the processes of education, training, and psychotherapy. Throughout this book readers are encouraged to engage critically with what I say, rather than simply accept it as authority; feminist practice cannot succeed unless the voices of all, including those officially defined as not-yet-authorities, are made authoritative. As I say to my supervisee in the companion DVD, "Yes, argue with me!" My hope is that your reading of this work will empower your own authority as you consider how to practice the feminist model of supervision.

1

Basic Principles of Feminist Supervision

This chapter reviews the history and foundational literature of feminist therapy theory. It introduces the reader to the constructs that are at the core of feminist supervision practice and explores what they mean when applied to supervisory work.

FEMINIST SUPERVISION

Definitions

I begin by defining *feminist therapy*:

> The practice of therapy informed by feminist political philosophies and analysis, grounded in multicultural feminist scholarship on the psychology of women and gender, which leads both therapist and client toward strategies and solutions advancing feminist resistance,

http://dx.doi.org/10.1037/14878-002
Supervision Essentials for the Feminist Psychotherapy Model of Supervision, by L. S. Brown

transformation and social change in daily personal life, and in relationships with the social, emotional and political environments.
(Brown, 1994, pp. 21–22)

This definition locates feminist therapy's origins in the study of women's experiences and highlights its specific interest in the topic of gender. Today, feminist therapy is a paradigm informing practice with humans of all genders (Brown, 2010) and is an explicitly multicultural model focused on how all aspects of identity converge intersectionally with nar-ratives of gender.

Feminist therapy *supervision* was formally defined by the Supervision Working Group of the 1993 National Conference on Education and Train-ing in Feminist Practice (Worell & Johnson, 1997). This conference brought together 77 leaders in the field of feminist psychology and psychotherapy who met in small groups to generate proposed guidelines for various aspects of feminist practice and then brought the proposals to the larger group for feedback and the development of consensus documents. This grassroots collective process reflects how feminist therapy theory and practice his-torically have developed and serves as a clue to the collective, collaborative nature of a feminist supervision relationship. The findings from this confer-ence have been generally accepted by feminist psychologists as informing practice across a range of spheres. Porter and Vasquez (1997) reported the definitions of feminist supervision from that conference as follows:

> Feminist supervision encompasses a collaborative relationship that is mutual and reflexive in nature. It is not egalitarian; rather, it is predicated on the principle of mutual respect characterized by clear, direct, and honest dialogic communication and responsible action. It encompasses awareness of and attention to the social, contextual nature of both the supervisory and the therapeutic processes. A femi-nist supervisory context embodies the feminist principles of ther-apy, including the analyses of power, boundaries, and hierarchy; an emphasis on social context and diversity; an examination of the rela-tionship of language to the social construction of gender; and the promotion of social activism, ethics, and lifelong self-examination and professional development. (p. 161)

Characteristics of Feminist Supervision

Supervision in the feminist paradigm embodies certain dynamic tensions between general ideals of feminist practice, such as egalitarian relationship and empowerment of the client, and realities of supervisory practice, such as supervisor legal responsibility for the work of supervisees and supervisor evaluative power. Falender (2010) noted,

> A challenge in clinical supervision is balancing tension between fostering a collaborative supervisory relationship and maintaining supervisory accountability. In feminist supervision this tension is heightened by virtue of its contextual, collaborative, and interpersonal qualities. What distinguishes feminist supervision from other models is the intent to address hierarchical factors and examine their impact rather than simply exercise the authority and the intent to honor the explicit commitment to the areas of mutuality possible in the relationship. Reflection and elaboration of tensions and potential conflicting roles are part of feminist supervisors' role definition. (p. 22)

Because of these tensions, a theme of this volume is the continuing interrogation of the role of supervisory power and questioning of means by which a feminist supervisory relationship can be closer to egalitarian. I argue, in contrast to Porter and Vasquez, that feminist supervision *can* be as egalitarian as feminist therapy. In each of these arrangements there are undeniable power dynamics. Yet in each, the person with the most role power (therapist, supervisor) can make choices that either aggravate the power imbalance or move it toward a position of greater equity; this emphasis on reducing power differentials, rather than an absence of power differentials, defines an egalitarian relationship.

As is discussed later in the review of feminist therapy theory, there has been a long confusion in feminist practice between the terms *egalitarian* and *equal*. No one would argue that feminist supervision is a relationship of equals—it is not and cannot be. Even feminist consultation is not entirely equal because one party is defined as being expert and the other is not. Despite the apparent inevitability of a hierarchical structure for supervision, I continuously suggest ways in which the feminist supervisor can disrupt whatever structural barriers to more equality are unnecessary for the safe and ethical practice of supervision. I examine and explore how the supervisor can structure a closer-to-egalitarian supervisory enterprise. I suggest that the more closely a feminist supervisory relationship comes to egalitarian, the easier it will be for the supervisee to grasp what it means to practice an egalitarian paradigm of psychotherapy or psychological assessment.

Purposeful collaboration between supervisor and supervisee to find solutions to the apparent contradiction between empowerment and evaluation inherent in the feminist supervisory situation is one of the distinguishing features of feminist supervision, as all parties strive to disrupt dominant culture discourses of what constitutes appropriate uses of power in educational and training contexts. Liberatory pedagogies (Freire, 1968) inform the feminist supervisor. The supervisor knows, as a feminist therapist, that the acts of psychotherapy or psychological assessment are in fact political ones, occurring in a larger social and political context, and are not simply professional transactions between a trainee therapist and a client. Teaching a trainee the politics of how language is used to describe distress or life challenges, how assessment instruments and strategies are chosen that will highlight strengths as well as deficits, and how psychotherapy can be structured that honors the differences and diversity in the room and situates that awareness in the realities of the larger social and political world—all of these are feminist and liberatory goals that differentiate feminist therapy supervision from general good psychotherapy supervision.

Porter and Vasquez (1997) described the characteristics of a feminist supervisor as follows:

> Feminist supervisors are proactive in analyzing power dynamics and differentials between the supervisor and the supervisee, model the use of power in the service of the supervisee, and vigilantly avoid abuses of power.
>
> Feminist supervision is based on a collaborative relationship, defined as mutually respectful, where the supervisee's autonomy and diverse perspectives are encouraged.

Feminist supervisors facilitate reflexive interactions and supervisee self-examination by modeling openness, authenticity, reflexivity, and the value of lifelong learning and self-examination.

Feminist supervision occurs in a social context that attends to and emphasizes the diversity of women's lives and contexts.

Feminist supervisors advance and model the feminist principles of advocacy and activism.

Feminist supervisors maintain standards that ensure their supervisees' competence and ethical practice.

Feminist supervisors attend to the developmental shifts occurring in the supervisory process and provide input as a function of the skill level, developmental level, and maturational level of the supervisee.

Feminist supervisors advocate for their supervisee and clients in the education and training setting within which they practice. (p. 170)

Note that some of these defining variables are simply those of good supervisors (e.g., attending to developmental shifts and trainee maturational level). Others are specifically feminist in their origins and reflect the activist roots of feminist therapy theory with its emphasis on attention to and analysis of power dynamics and imbalances.

Gentile, Ballou, Roffman, and Ritchie (2009) argued for an expanded purview of what constitutes feminist supervision, suggesting that such supervision must adopt an ecological model of human behavior and experience (Ballou, Matsumoto, & Wagner, 2002) that addresses not simply the individual experiences of power and disempowerment but also explicitly attends to the effects of the larger sociopolitical context in which clients, therapists, and supervisors function and with which they interact.

These authors provided examples of ways in which a feminist supervisor can offer opportunities for making justice in larger social structures in which trainees are working, such as courts or schools. They also reminded feminist supervisors that justice begins in the supervisory relationship. Ballou and her colleagues noted that "supervisory relationships provide a place to reflect on justice making . . . Qualities of fair treatment in these (supervisory) relationships parallel and mirror the qualities of social justice in the larger social context" (Gentile et al., 2009, p. 150). They underscored the notion that feminist supervision is distinctive from other models in its explicit emphasis on not only promoting social justice practice but also having the goal of *being* a social justice practice.

Thus, feminist perspectives in supervision can be seen as embracing a wide range of possibilities for supervisors and those being supervised. The emphasis is on the integration of feminist knowledge and principles of empowerment, justice, and social change into the experience of the trainee psychotherapist. Supervision is construed not simply as a means of teaching psychological practice, but also as a vehicle for conscious raising, personal awareness, and self-reflexivity regarding dynamics of gender and power and self-development as a feminist and therapist. The trainee in feminist supervision does not simply learn how to practice psychotherapy or psychological assessment; she or he also learns to critically examine norms of diagnosis, ethics, and psychotherapy practice and develop a model of psychological practice that is liberatory as well as healing.

TEACH OR TREAT OR EMPOWER? *intended to teach*

A common question found in many discussions of supervision theory is whether supervision is a primarily intellectual exercise of a didactic nature or one in which explorations of the person of the trainee therapist can move perilously close to psychotherapeutic interventions with the trainee. Feminist models of supervision eschew this dichotomy and instead ask the question "What will *empower* this particular trainee to the most effective level of practice and competence?" Feminist models are developmentally informed, attending to the emotional and experiential realities of the person being supervised, and collaborative, in that the supervisor and supervisee enter into a shared understanding of the goals of supervision.

 *abstain from*

What is important in this model is that the person with less formal power, the supervisee, be availed of full informed consent to the supervisory process and take ownership of what will occur. If and when supervision moves heavily into explorations of supervisee countertransference, and thus personal material, this direction for supervision should take place in a manner that empowers the trainee. If the demand characteristics of the supervision are such that a trainee feels unsafe, disempowered, or shamed by a move toward this kind of material, a violation of feminist ethics has occurred (Dutton & Rave, 1990).

However, this does not mean that a trainee will not experience brief moments of shame or temporary disempowerment or distress in the service of empathy with clients. Rather, the implication is that in feminist supervision, there is clear consent to engage in this level of depth exploration by the trainee. The supervisor will not impose a requirement on a trainee to engage in process supervision without clear consent and will instead collaborate with the trainee when proposing this methodology, exploring the risks and benefits, and will not pathologize a trainee's decisions about where to set privacy boundaries. A feminist supervisor with this type of goal for supervision should be prepared to use self-disclosure liberally in the service of modeling the sort of self-reflexivity that is required of the supervisee and as a means of reducing the power imbalances that arise from depth work with a supervisee.

The following scenario may help illustrate this. A supervisee reports being stuck in his work with a client. The supervisor engages, challenges, and asks questions, and the supervisee's body language changes to a position of shame. Tears emerge. "I'm having such strong countertransference with this person; I feel as if I'm in the room with my grandfather again. What's wrong with me that I can't get past this?"

This scenario is one common to all models of supervision. Psychotherapists are challenged by the appearance in their offices of people who evoke strong, and usually painful, emotional resonances with the difficult and important people of their own pasts. Many psychotherapists are "wounded healers" (Bryan, 2012), yet most training experiences in the mental health fields attempt to obscure this reality, often shaming people for having the histories that both inform their choice to become therapists and create their particular vulnerabilities in working with certain clients.

Self-disclosure by the supervisor can be one effective empowerment strategy at these junctures. As I discuss later in this book, feminist therapy theory creates an explicit framework supporting its use in therapy and, by association, in supervision. The therapist's willingness to disclose her or his own struggles with mood, trauma, and the ghosts of difficult people past in her or his therapeutic work can normalize the trainee's experience and reframe it as a source of competence and capacity rather than as a problem.

In the example above, a feminist supervisor might begin by framing the trainee's willingness to be transparent as a form of competence, offering the feminist diagnostic model of vulnerability and transparency as forms of interpersonal powerfulness. The supervisor might then offer to the trainee examples of parallel experiences in the supervisor's recent work, exposing the reality that powerful countertransferential responses to clients are not evidence of inexperience as a psychotherapist but rather universals that emerge repeatedly during the course of one's work (Pope & Tabachnick, 1993), or share other personal or professional experiences of struggle that mirror those being experienced by the trainee. My application of this construct is illustrated by the supervision case example derived from the video, which is discussed at length later as I discuss the supervisee's feelings of rejection and anger in relationship to some of her clients.

Thus, feminist supervision is both teach *and* treat, as agreed to by the supervisory pair, in a collaborative context in which trainee rights to privacy boundaries are explicitly respected and in the interest of the empowerment of the person being supervised. It is always, whether didactic or process oriented, focused on empowerment of the supervisee. Feminist supervision assumes that a supervisee will be less able to empower clients if she or he is not explicitly empowered in the supervision process.

A BRIEF HISTORY OF FEMINIST THERAPY THEORY

Feminist supervisory and consultative practice requires the supervisor or consultant to understand the development of the field and to have adopted and internalized the principles of feminist therapy practice. One cannot practice feminist supervision if one is not both a feminist and a feminist therapist, and the more closely a supervisor adheres to feminist therapy constructs, the more likely that the supervisor will score high on measures of feminist supervision, irrespective of any personal characteristics or experience in supervision. The remainder of this chapter reviews the principles of feminist theory and practice.

Feminist therapy has its original clinical roots in the humanistic psychotherapies that were practiced by many of its initial adherents before their engagement with the women's movement at the end of the 1960s. The "third force" psychotherapies that emerged strongly during the 1960s were experienced by many women practitioners as offering a viable alternative to what was seen as the determinism and misogyny of psychoanalysis and the mechanistic view of humans that then defined behaviorism.

Eventually the founders of feminist therapy also found the humanistic psychotherapies to be insufficient as a framework for understanding their experiences, particularly as those women joined feminist consciousness-raising (CR) groups and began to have a critique of gender relations in the humanistic psychotherapy movements. Fisher (1981) noted that "CR envisions the liberation of the self, or rather, of a part of the self which is denied by the oppressive conditions under which we live" (p. 22). The self that was liberated for many early feminist psychologists was the critical self, the self that questioned the authority of psychology as a masculinist and misogynist enterprise and that gave voice to the experiences of women through their own lens.

The intersection of CR with the lives of psychotherapists was the catalyst for the emergence of a specifically feminist commentary on the practice of psychotherapy (Chesler, 1972; Rawlings & Carter, 1977). In CR groups, women met together without a leader and shared personal experiences of their lives, including experiences of discrimination. Participating in these groups, the original feminist therapists began to notice themes and trends common to many women's lives and, in particular, common to their particular experiences of being trained as psychotherapists and being clients in psychotherapy. In parallel with raised consciousness about sexism and misogyny in the culture at large, an awareness of these pervasive biases in the psychotherapy profession emerged. Because they were listening to other women describe parallel experiences, feminists in the psychotherapy professions became empowered to take steps to change their own disciplines (Rosewater & Walker, 1985).

As a separate model of psychotherapy, feminist therapy in psychology has its most traceable conceptual origins in three documents. These documents can be said to have functioned as large-scale, consciousness-raising tools for the psychotherapists who read them. Many of the first generation of feminist therapists mark the moment of their epiphany-like association with feminist therapy to reading one or more of these pieces of literature (Brown, 1994; Cole, Rothblum, & Chesler, 1995; Kaschak, 1992).

These three pieces were Chesler's *Women and Madness* (1972); Weisstein's *Kinder, Kuche, Kirche as Scientific Law: Psychology Constructs the Female* (1968); and *Sex-Role Stereotypes and Clinical Judgments of Mental Health* by Broverman, Broverman, Clarkson, Rosenkrantz, and Vogel (1970). Each of these documents presaged developments to follow in the emergence of feminist therapy's theory and practice.

Weisstein's (1968) essay was a masterful critique of the sexism and misogyny inherent in psychological science, particularly the tiny amount of psychology that had attended to sex and gender. Broverman and her colleagues empirically demonstrated that, for the experienced psychotherapist practicing before 1972, the mentally healthy human was different from the mentally healthy woman but not the mentally healthy man. Their findings confirmed the experience of women who had been in therapy that a double standard existed for how women and men were treated by their therapists. Finally, Chesler's (1972) *tour de force* documented the pervasive effects of these misogynist and sexist dynamics when applied to the lives of real women in the psychotherapy process. She drew the parallels between gendered hierarchies in the larger culture and similar hierarchies of power and dominance between male psychotherapists and their female clients and exposed the phenomenon of sexual exploitation of clients by therapists. For their readers, these writings had the effect of initiating the first step in any process of feminist therapy, which is the arousal of feminist consciousness in the individual, a consciousness without which feminist practice cannot occur.

Lerner (1993) defined *feminist consciousness* as the development of awareness that one's maltreatment is not due to individual deficits but to membership in a group that has been unfairly subordinated. Feminist consciousness also states that society can and should be changed to give equal power and value to all. Specifically as to feminism within the psychotherapy professions, this consciousness took the form of understanding that almost all of what had been written about women before 1970 was distorted by misogynist bias that was then taken as scientific wisdom about women, who were defined as lesser varieties of men.

For the founders of feminist therapy, consciousness raising highlighted the reality that the practice of psychotherapy was steeped in oppressive norms and values that were harmful to women. In many instances, this epiphany was accompanied by a cognitive reappraisal of personal experiences with sexist and misogynist psychotherapy or professional relationships. In these reevaluations, feminist psychologists realized that the difficulties they had encountered were not evidence of personal deficit, inadequacy, or neurosis but instead were reflections of the unabashed sexism of the other person or the situation. Feminists who were psychotherapists noted the powerful effects of this raised consciousness on their own well-being.

Feminism teaches that "the personal is political." For this group of early feminist therapists and feminist psychologists, the development of feminist consciousness and politics arose from their own experiences as graduate students, therapists, and sometimes clients within the patriarchal system of psychotherapy as practiced universally before the early 1970s (Baker Miller & Welch, 1995; Bernardez, 1995; Caplan, 1995; Cole, Rothblum, & Chesler, 1995; Denmark, 1995; Gartrell, 1995; Greenspan, 1995). For Phyllis Chesler and Naomi Weisstein, the experiences of sexism and discrimination in their professional settings were the specific catalyst for their groundbreaking written work. Examining psychology and psychotherapy from within, Chesler and Weisstein each applied the tools of critical analysis and scientific method in which they had been trained in their doctoral educations and found the field sorely wanting.

Feminist supervisors, especially those educated in more recent time periods when the pervasive and overt sexism that Chesler and Weisstein identified has gone underground and become more implicit, need to be familiar with these founding documents and with the historical context in which feminist practice arose in psychology and related professions. Without this historical perspective, it can be more difficult to appreciate the value of an explicitly feminist perspective on psychotherapy and supervision; given the degree to which so many of the early methodologies of feminist therapy have been adopted into what is considered good practice, the feminist roots of those methodologies have been made invisible. An in-depth review of this material can be found in Brown (2010).

In the initial decades of its development, feminist therapy theory and practice occurred almost entirely outside of formal academic settings, at conferences and meetings called by practitioners seeking community and connection with other self-identified feminist therapists. Feminist psychologists were unlikely to get academic jobs or tenure in psychology until the end of the 20th century. Professional organizations, such as the Association for Women in Psychology, the Feminist Therapy Institute, the Section for the Advancement of Women of the Society of Counseling Psychology, and the Society for the Psychology of Women, arose as resources for feminist psychological science, scholarship, and the development of norms for practice. A rich literature on feminist psychological practice has emerged from these organizations; feminist supervisors must be familiar with this literature. Because many of the problems of sexism and misogyny identified four decades ago at the inception of feminist practice have not disappeared, but have rather become more subtle and thus potentially more difficult to identify and address, feminist supervisors need to be adept in identifying such dynamics in the supervisory context and in the work of the trainees they are supervising.

KEY CONCEPTS IN FEMINIST THERAPY THEORY

Feminist therapy, and as such feminist supervision, is informed by several key concepts. Because feminist therapy theory is considered superordinate to any specific intervention, understanding these concepts is fundamental to effective feminist supervisory practice. The concepts are: the egalitarian relationship, analysis of power, and the centrality of understanding social constructions of gender and other aspects of identities in comprehending the distress that brings people to therapy.

The Egalitarian Relationship

At the heart of feminist therapy lies the *egalitarian relationship*, the interpersonal context of psychotherapy in which empowerment is gestated (Brown, 1994, 2010; Faunce, 1985; Greenspan, 1982; Smith & Siegel, 1985). Not a relationship of equals, it is instead a paradigm for equal value and for seeing each participant as an expert who brings a particular set of skills and knowledge to the collaboration. As therapy progresses, the power imbalance should lessen as the client comes to increasingly own her or his authority as an expert agent in her or his life.

Feminist therapy theory acknowledges that there is an inevitable imbalance of power in therapeutic and supervisory relationships. Rather than simply accepting this power imbalance as unassailable status quo, feminist therapy theory has offered systemic strategies for minimizing that imbalance, never ignoring the legal and ethical norms for practice and never denying the power of the psychotherapist or supervisor. In the social system that is the psychotherapy or supervisory relationship, feminist practice strives to shift privilege and authority to the voice, knowing, and experiences of those receiving services, instead of only acknowledging the authority of the psychotherapist or supervisor.

The egalitarian relationship ideal suffered much at first from "egalitarian" and "equal" having the same Latin roots. The process of developing a clear model of egalitarianism in psychotherapy was challenged by attempts to differentiate egalitarian and equal. The Feminist Therapy Institute's Code of Ethics was developed in the context of this particular dilemma and is important reading for all feminist therapists who are striving to be egalitarian, responsible, and boundaried. Its wording on what constitutes egalitarian ethical practice reflects the understanding that the therapist (and also supervisor), by virtue of role, has greater role power in the relationship and holds responsibility for delineation and maintenance of boundaries while also having a responsibility to empower clients (and trainees) within that other-than-equal framework (Feminist Therapy Institute, 1990, 1995, 1999).

Because supervision in feminist therapy does not construct egalitarianism in the same manner as in therapy, a feminist supervisor must be able to comprehend and practice egalitarian relationship in her or his psychotherapeutic work so as to have an experiential foundation for this practice and to model it to trainees. She or he is then tasked with navigating a supervisory relationship that is in process toward egalitarianism as the trainee's capacities grow and mature. Just as a feminist therapist holds a vision of clients as whole, healed, and empowered, so the feminist supervisor holds a vision of the trainee as a junior colleague who will emerge into equal role status and to whom she or he will be able to confidently refer at some time in the not too distant future.

Visualizing the trainee as her or his fully equal future self and making this vision explicit in feminist supervision lends a tone of respect and mutuality to the supervisory relationship even though the realities of the supervisor's evaluative power are undeniably present. I repeatedly tell trainees that I see them as my junior colleagues and strive to treat them as such. As a feminist supervisor, I attempt to use my evaluative powers in the supervisory relationship to support their growth into being my colleague in ways that will strengthen our relationships for the future.

Analysis of Power Dynamics

To empower, a therapist and supervisor must have a sophisticated understanding of what constitutes power. In feminist therapy theory, power is not defined in the usual way—that is, having control of other humans and/or resources. Instead, it is construed as the capacity to have impact on oneself and others and to be freed from dominant cultural memes (e.g., ideas, behaviors, or styles that spread from person to person within a culture) that assign differential value to humans based on gender, sex, phenotype, sexuality, age, ability, ethnicity, immigration status, religious identification, or other identity variables (Brown, 2010). Feminist supervision attempts to empower supervisees in ways similar to those used in feminist therapy. In addition, feminist supervision offers the didactic component of teaching trainees to understand how feminist therapy precepts are put into practice.

Feminist supervision starts with the assumption that both the supervisor and the supervisee have experienced power and disempowerment throughout life, either because of positions in social hierarchies or because of individualized experiences, such as trauma. Feminist supervision models assume that these experiences of power and disempowerment affect the supervisory process and the therapy being supervised. Disempowerment and the biopsychosocial and/or existential consequences of powerlessness are construed by feminist therapy theory as central sources of emotional distress and behavioral dysfunction. Feminist therapy asks, generally and specifically, what might constitute a move toward power for a given person in the domains where powerlessness has been experienced. The feminist therapist is tasked with the cocreation with her or his client of strategies that invite and support empowerment for each person. For a supervisor to practice feminist supervision, she or he must develop a nuanced and sophisticated understanding of the feminist analysis of power and, in parallel to the questions asked of clients about the small steps toward empowerment, engage trainees to see the increasing number of ways in which they may be empowered.

This analysis of power dynamics is central to the development of egalitarian models of relating and also is a core component of how interventions are structured by feminist practitioners. Feminist therapy theory encourages its practitioners to attend to issues of privilege (e.g., unearned social power and access to human and material resources deriving from one's location in social hierarchies; McIntosh, 1998) as useful information about power dynamics.

As a supervisor, one holds the privilege in the supervisory relationship, regardless of how privilege in distributed outside the room. Consequently, the supervisor must be highly attuned to ways in which she or he exerts subtle influence and own her or his power in the role; this can be particularly challenging when the trainee's privilege is greater in larger social realities (e.g., Euro American trainee, supervisor of color; upper class trainee, supervisor from poverty-class background). The feminist supervisor remains cognizant of the ways in which all parties' multiple and intersecting identities outside of the supervisory relationship can distribute privilege in ways that are both challenged and intensified by the distribution of power in formal supervision.

An important component of the feminist supervisory relationship with regard to dynamics of privilege is the supervisor's capacity for mindful and self-compassionate reflexivity with regard to her or his privilege relative to that of the persons being supervised, with particular attention to the privilege inherent in the evaluative role of the supervisor. Because the feminist supervisory relationship is structured to empower trainees in ways somewhat different from how psychotherapy is structured to empower clients, analysis of power dynamics in supervision both resembles and is different from that in feminist psychotherapy.

Feminist supervisors consequently introduce awareness and discussions of privilege and power into the supervisory environment, putting both the therapy being practiced and the supervision of that therapy under scrutiny for ways in which power imbalances, particularly those that are not immediately identifiable, become manifest. They invite trainees to understand how multiple and intersecting identities lead to variable experiences of privilege and disadvantage and model, for trainees, the exploration of those intersectionalities in the supervisory relationship (Feminist Therapy Institute, 1990, 1995). They use their role privilege to empower trainees via emphasis on competence while supporting growth at the edges of that competence and naming clear failures of competence should they occur in either party.

Here is an example. I was supervising a postdoctoral trainee when a conflict arose between her and a client regarding ways in which the client was asking the therapist to relate on the client's behalf to a third party. The client's words and actions (she accused the therapist of unethical behavior and considered filing a complaint against the therapist, who was practicing under my license and supervision) were intensely emotionally activating for me, leading me to become uncharacteristically and anxiously controlling with my trainee. Based on our relationship, the trainee was empowered to confront me about my failure of supervision, which was engendering anxiety in her rather than assisting her to manage the rupture repair with her client. I appreciated her actively for that challenge, and we used our own rupture repair as a strategy for exploring the parallel process in the psychotherapy.

Collaborative Relationship

Feminist therapy theory counsels collaboration with recipients of services on goals for the relationship, both the broad overarching ones and the specifics of a given encounter. Thus, a feminist therapist or supervisor must be responsive and flexible so as to meet clients or trainees where they are, personally and developmentally, empowering the recipients of services to their optimal levels of capacity. Although a given feminist practitioner may have a strong bias toward a particular model for intervention or training (e.g., cognitive–behavioral therapy or relational psychoanalysis), she or he must always be integrating that model into the overarching goal of empowerment of the person receiving services and the exploration of gendered dynamics. Feminist practice does not strongly support the use of purely manualized treatments that fail to account for the effects of gender, ethnicity, social class, and other identity variables on the presenting problem or on the psychotherapy context and is critical of psychotherapy research that fails to take diversity into account. As a supervisor, the feminist practitioner models flexibility, an integrative mind-set, and openness to working in ways that empower, rather than undermine, the agency and sense of efficacy of the recipient of services. The goal of the feminist supervisor is not to reproduce in its entirety her or his own way of doing therapy. Rather, it is to induce in trainees the capacity to understand and more fully develop their ways of being psychotherapists within the integrative framework that is feminist practice. Later I discuss several considerations for deepening one's understanding of the manifestations of power dynamics in psychotherapy and supervision.

Power Dynamics in Therapy: Symbolic Relationships

Historically, feminist therapy has not formally used the construct of a transference relationship as conceptualized by psychodynamic psychotherapies.

However, feminist therapy, as biopsychosocial/existential paradigm, affirms the reality that each person in the relationship represents both the real here-and-now and also symbolizes something to the other person in both conscious and other-than-conscious ways that are both like and larger than transference and countertransference. The more common terminology is now used more readily by many feminist therapists with the understanding that the feminist understanding of these dynamics encompasses more than nonconscious phenomena based solely in early experiences in families of origin. Feminist therapy theory posits that there are individual and socio-political transferences and countertransferences. "When and where I enter, there and then the whole race enters with me," said Anna Julia Cooper, the 19th-century African American suffrage activist (Giddings, 1996); this aphorism guides feminist practitioners in understanding how they may symbolically represent to those receiving their services. Feminist supervisors impart this construct of "transference/countertransference plus" to trainees.

Feminist therapy theory consequently attends to how symbolic personal and cultural phenomena and as current social realities evoke nonconscious representations that affect the balance of power in the relationship. For the feminist supervisor, this entails a continuous attention to the manifest and nonconscious realms and the here-and-now interaction between those realms. This topic is discussed at greater length in Chapter 4, which explores diversity and multicultural concerns in feminist supervision.

Use of Self-Disclosure

Feminist therapists also use a number of structural and ecological strategies in their practices to systemically decrease imbalances of power and increase similarities of access to resources in therapy. Although none of these are prescribed or required strategies for a feminist therapist, they are among the ones most frequently referred to in feminist therapy literature. Consistent with the research on positive effects of self-disclosure (Hill & Knox, 2002), as well as with its roots in humanistic models valuing therapist genuineness (Rogers, 1957), feminist therapy, with its roots in the powerful shared experiences of CR, has long supported therapist self-disclosure in the client's interest (Brown, 1991, 1994, 2010; Brown &

Walker, 1990; Feminist Therapy Institute, 1990, 1995, 1999) as an empowerment strategy. Consequently, feminist supervision will most commonly entail the use of self-disclosure as well as exploration with trainees about how they can apply it within their therapeutic frame. I find that teaching from my own missteps and stumbles not only illuminates the unpredictable realities of psychotherapy practice to trainees, but also empowers them to become more transparent and willing to risk being closely observed in supervision.

Nonneutrality

Feminist therapy theory asserts that there is no such thing as a neutral or objective psychotherapist, noting that so-called objectivity is what the person with the most power calls her own subjectivity. The feminist paradigm posits that those who refuse to acknowledge the reality that they have a standpoint or perspectives, or deny that they would be affected by who and how a client is, are more likely to act out their disowned biases and thereby risk increasing power differentials. While a feminist therapist exercises personal discretion as to how and where her or his privacy boundaries are set, the therapist must be self-reflexive and attuned to the distinct possibility that information that is not overtly disclosed in the name of remaining apparently neutral may be transparent to the person with less power in the relationship and have other-than-neutral effects. A ring on the "wedding ring" finger, the cut of one's clothes, whether the rug on the floor is a Macy's knock-off or a genuine Persian: each personal choice made by a therapist telegraphs something about the therapist's identity.

Thus, self-reflexivity about aversive (nonconscious) bias (Dovidio, Gaertner, Kawakami, & Hodson, 2002), which frequently develops in a context of privilege, is essential for feminist practice and the empowerment of those receiving the services of feminist practitioners. A feminist practitioner knows that she or he has bias. Rather than experiencing shame or guilt over this departure from neutrality, the feminist practitioner strives to acknowledge bias and make choices not to enact it. The feminist practitioner also is aware of ways in which she or he evokes aversive bias from clients and supervisees and uses that awareness in the service of the relationship.

Egalitarian Business Practices

Feminist therapy theory extends its understanding of egalitarian strategies to the details of the therapist's business practices, including where an office is situated in terms of its accessibility to a range of diverse clients and various strategies of communication about inclusion or exclusion, how a therapist prefers to be addressed (e.g., am I "Dr. Brown" or am I "Laura," and who decides; is my client "Ms. Hernandez" or "Anita," and who decides), and how fees are set (Brown, 1991, 1994, 2007, 2010; Luepnitz, 1988). Feminist supervision consequently includes discussions of these matters as an aspect of professional development for the trainee, whether or not the trainee is dealing with business practices at a particular point in professional development. If the supervisor and supervisee have a business relationship, it is structured to be just, not simply adopting whatever model of percentage of gross is a norm.

Distress, Dysfunction, and Resistance: Feminist Diagnosis as Empowerment Strategy

Formal diagnosis is a topic with which feminist therapy historically has had a deeply conflicted, highly critical, and ambivalent relationship. Instruction regarding analysis of oppressive memes in formal diagnosis is an important component of feminist supervision. Early feminist therapists avoided the use of formal diagnosis, and many feminist therapists continue to avoid it when possible. Feminist therapy theory conceives of formal diagnosis as a disempowering reification, objectification, and pathologizing of the strategies used by oppressed and disempowered individuals for increasing personal power by whatever means available (Ballou & Brown, 2000). In addition, feminists and other critical psychological theorists have critiqued the lack of scientific rigor in the psychiatric diagnostic systems, noting the high level of influence from the psychopharmacological industry and the politics that historically have infused those tasked with creating diagnostic manuals.

Nonetheless, many feminist therapists practice in settings in which the use of formal diagnosis is required, and feminist supervisors are almost always tasked by the training programs from which supervisees come with schooling trainees in the use of formal diagnosis. To manage this conundrum, feminist supervisors model discussing formal diagnoses with clients when the assignment of a diagnosis is necessary and collaborating with clients on arriving at a diagnosis that makes sense to clients and reflects their phenomenological experiences of distress. Feminist supervision actively teaches this strategy for approaching the diagnostic process to trainees as a means of encouraging critical thinking about formal diagnosis and offering empowerment-based alternatives for relating to diagnostic manuals, including introducing trainees to the feminist and critical literature about diagnosis.

Distress and *behavioral dysfunction* are terms proposed by feminist therapists in preference to the word *psychopathology* (Ballou & Brown, 2000; Brown & Ballou, 1992). As Brown and Ballou (1992) noted,

> . . . we see that the decision to call nonconforming thoughts, values, and actions psychopathology does two things. First, it discounts she or he who is described as such. Second, it blocks our ability to look outside the individual to see forces, dynamics, and structure that influence the development of such thinking, values and actions. (p. xviii)

Pathology is construed instead as a systemic variable, residing in oppressive hierarchies of power and dominance, rather than as an individual variable located in the person. The strategy of externalizing the basis of a client's problems and distress while identifying and empowering the client to become the agent who can solve those problems is a reset of the locus of responsibility. The goal is a shifting of responsibility for the toxic effects of powerful and oppressive social forces off the shoulders of an individual in distress and back into the lap of the persons and institutions from which that betrayal and disempowerment emanated. This message that "you are not the problem, and you *are* the solution" as a paradigm for conceptualizing distress is central to feminist practice and thus an important component of what is conveyed by feminist supervisors in discussing case conceptualizations with supervisees.

Specific symptoms of distress and dysfunction are construed by feminist therapy theory as evidence of attempts to resist the effects of oppression, betrayal, and disempowerment, and to solve the problem of powerlessness and its painful affects via whatever means are available biologically, developmentally, intrapsychically, contextually, culturally, and/or spiritually in that moment (Brown, 1994, 2010).

Feminist therapy theory posits that all persons make attempts to solve the problems of their existence, but that not all strategies work as well or as persistently as others, and that some strategies require access to resources that are dependent on privilege that is unevenly distributed and frequently unavailable. This paradigm of person-as-active-problem-solver is used in feminist practice in preference to the pathology model for understanding psychological distress and is one of the constructs conveyed to trainees by feminist supervision.

Feminist therapy theory acknowledges that some experiences of distress have strong biological components and origins. However, it argues that how even the most biologically generated distress is culturally received and coded and the metadistress that a person and the person's social context has about the symptom have as much if not more impact on the degree of distress that a person perceives. This meta-appraisal of the meaning of the symptom (e.g., "I am being blessed by a Divine being" vs. "I am crazy and losing my mind") also informs how a person behaves in response to his or her inner experiences. Most forms of psychosis are now considered to most likely be attributable in large part to the expressions of as-yet-unidentified biological variables that affect a person's neurochemistry. Nonetheless, the manner in which the culture responds to experiences labeled as psychotic has much to do with how much distress will occur as a result of those experiences.

This perspective on atypical experiences of reality reflects an embedding of appraisals of those experiences in historical and cultural contexts. A close reading of the lives of many saints, biblical prophets, and founders of world religions suggests that all or most experienced what today would be called some form of psychosis or delusional thinking. In their cultures and their times, they were valued as women and men of vision and holiness, not diagnosed psychotic, locked away, or medicated. They often were distressed by their inner experiences, and yet they did not have the metadistress of appraising themselves as insane or the universal disempowerment accorded to psychotic persons by dominant 21st-century cultures.

Feminist supervision offers this viewpoint to trainees, disrupting the "this person must take antipsychotic medication or be seen as non-compliant" narrative that currently is dominant. This is not an anti-medication stance; rather, the feminist supervisor invites trainees to critically interrogate the current narrative about the risks and benefits of psychiatric medications and ally with clients' preferences when possible.

Feminist therapists pay attention to the larger social context as it influences the experiences of distress clients bring into therapy, the ways in which clients express that distress, and the process of therapy itself. Feminist therapists invite clients to attend to ways in which the external environment has been a source of misinformation about themselves, their value, and their capacities. They ask themselves and their clients to examine how culture has taught them to encode their inner experiences into communications with the world; how has someone learned to convey sadness, fear, and anger when all of those emotions, and more, are constrained in their expression by norms of gender and culture? They also invite clients and themselves to notice how changing external worlds affect internal and relational worlds, changing the salience of an experience to render it more meaningful in either joyful or painful ways. The client in feminist therapy is thus empowered to think of her or his distress differently and to coconstruct its meanings with the therapist, rather than accept labels applied by alleged experts. Feminist supervision engages trainees to apply this transformative paradigm of psychological distress in their clinical work.

All of these strategies factor into the creation of egalitarian relationships that are the foundation of feminist practice. However, simply attending to power dynamics is necessary, but not sufficient, for a therapy to be feminist. Analysis of gender and related social locations and identities is another necessary component.

Analysis of Gender and Intersectionalities of Identity

For feminist therapy, understanding and critical analysis of constructions of gender as they have been experienced by an individual takes a central place in theorizing human development. The notion that rigid narratives of gender are major contributors to the development of psychological distress is a central tenet of feminist therapy theory. Feminist therapy theory focuses on how constructions of the gendered self become sources of power or disempowerment that later inform the difficulties for which people seek therapy (Ballou & Brown, 2000; Kaschak, 1992; Lerman, 1996). Feminist psychological science has demonstrated the pervasiveness with which cultures conflate sex (biology) and gender (socially constructed narratives), and the resistance, both in society at large and among professionals, to empirical data challenging the immutability of the gendering of characteristics and talents (Hyde, 2005).

Gendered Behavior as an Artifact of Power

Unger (1989) experimentally manipulated the variables of sex and power for the participants in a group problem-solving dilemma. Her findings are provocative. When women in the group were placed in the powerful role as defined by the experimenter, their expressed behavior resembled characteristics that are gendered masculine in U.S. culture. Men placed in the subordinate position behaved consistent with so-called feminine attributes. Although it is not surprising, given women's historical oppression in global patriarchies, that the experience of subordination has become conflated with sex, it is intriguing and informative to observe how quickly social position and disempowerment can overcome gendered socialization even in the brief context of the social psychology experiment.

Gender role analysis as a specific technique of feminist therapy (Worell & Remer, 2003) is one of the original tools of feminist practice. More recently, analysis of other identity variables, such as culture, phenotype, social class, sexual orientation, disability, ethnicity, age, linguistic and immigration status, and spiritual orientation, have been integrated into this model (Brown, 2010). Doing gender role analysis takes the discussion of gender's social constructions into account, allowing the therapist to consider how her or his experiences and those of the client are informed by gender. Unpacking and making transparent the assumptions about sex and gender, including notions of gender as a binary or essential phenomenon, that are profoundly rooted in cultural norms can be an effective feminist empowerment strategy.

Implicit in these discussions of gender and other identity variables is that, because they are sources of power and powerlessness, they are also factors in the development of distress and dysfunction because of the inextricable linkage of gender with sexism, misogyny, and other forms of bias and oppression.

THE ROLE OF EVALUATION IN FEMINIST SUPERVISION AND CONSULTATION

Although feminist therapy practice tends to rely heavily on client feedback as the gold standard for determining success of the enterprise, supervision and consultation in feminist therapy are distinctly different from psychotherapy with regard to how outcome is evaluated. This is entirely because of the training functions of supervision (and, to a lesser degree, consultation). Feminist supervisors are training therapists for future practice or consulting with less-experienced colleagues. Consequently, there is a gatekeeping responsibility held by the feminist supervisor: a responsibility to the welfare of the public and to the supervisee's current and future clients. For the supervision of graduate students, the supervisor also has a legal relationship with the student's training program.

In the case of formal supervision of practicum, internship, or postdoctoral training, the supervised person practices under the license of the supervisor. The supervisor consequently holds formal ethical and legal responsibility for the clients being treated by the supervisee. A consultant, although not legally responsible, is ethically responsible to the consultee and her or his clients and must be attuned to the possibility of consultee impairment and aware of laws mandating report of impaired practitioners. Thus, supervisee or consultee satisfaction with the process is not the sine qua non of excellent feminist supervision or consultation; a supervisee or consultee who is being strenuously challenged or confronted about subpar quality of her or his work or being disciplined by a supervisor is not likely to be entirely satisfied with what is occurring.

This necessary authority in the role of the feminist supervisor creates additional and interesting challenges that are specific to feminist practice. The feminist supervisor seeks to develop an egalitarian relationship with the supervisee and yet must retain the authority to protect clients, be directive as needed, and develop educational and disciplinary consequences for a supervisee who is struggling to practice wisely or safely. The feminist supervisor must figure out how to assess the trustworthiness of a trainee, knowing that a trainee's misconduct redounds to the harm of the supervisor and any affected client. All supervisors and consultants have these sorts of ethical, legal, and moral responsibilities. However, most models of training and psychotherapy do not expect the supervisor to also find ways to explicitly empower the person being supervised and develop an egalitarian relationship with that individual. Balancing egalitarianism with the powers inherent in and necessary for the tasks of supervision and, to a lesser degree, consultation creates a unique conundrum for feminist supervisors that is discussed at length in sections of this book addressing dealing with impaired and problematic supervisees.

The feminist supervisor also has an indirect relationship with the client involved. This is true in all supervision; in feminist supervision, the supervisor's invisible presence in the room is made more explicit than in most models aside from family psychotherapy practiced with the supervisor behind the mirror. The client's empowerment, satisfaction with the process and outcomes of psychotherapy, and perspectives on what does and does not work for him or her enter the frame of feminist supervision in an explicit and perhaps unique manner. All supervisors and consultants should be taking into account the values and preferences of their supervisee's clients. However, feminist supervision uniquely defines clients as additional experts and implicit members of the supervision team. Taking the client into account in supervision in an egalitarian and empowering manner is yet another facet of feminist supervision that may differentiate it from other supervisory models. One of my most frequent responses to trainees asking what they should do next is, "Why don't you ask your client and collaborate with her/him?"

However, the need to evaluate does not free a feminist supervisor from including supervisee's assessments of outcome in estimates of whether a supervision experience has been successful. Disciplinary actions, which are discussed at length in Chapter 4, need not depart from an egalitarian and empowering paradigm. The challenge for feminist supervisors is to develop disciplinary strategies that remain true to feminist ideals. In fact, this theory-driven function of feminist practice, the empowerment of the recipient of services and the reliance on the voice and perspective of the recipient to evaluate outcome, implies that assessment in supervision is a bidirectional, not unilateral, process. That is, the feminist supervisor gives feedback and structures ways in which to receive it and also models openness to input from the person with less formal power in the relationship.

Patriarchy and Disempowerment in Supervision

I proposed (Brown, 2010) a model of power as a four-axial phenomenon. I argue that empowerment and disempowerment can occur in the realms of intrapsychic and intrapersonal experiences, interpersonal interactions, relationships to the body, and with regard to existential and meaning-making systems.

Feminist therapy asserts that the patriarchal systems that dominate human societies function so as to intentionally and unintentionally disempower almost all people on one or more of these variables. However, feminist theory argues that much powerlessness can be transformed, even within the material constraints of patriarchal realities, and that one disempowerment strategy of patriarchies has been the creation of a trance of powerlessness that is both cultural and personal, in which various messages are conveyed that most people can never have power. Feminist supervision pays particular attention to the dynamics of disempowerment in the psychotherapy training process, a matter discussed at greater length later in this book.

The wide-scale disempowering messages conveyed by patriarchies about the inevitability of hierarchies, the impossibility of effecting real social change, the impossibility of attaining access to resources, and the immutability of gendered and other socially constructed roles and relationships all contribute to this societal trance, which in turn permeates the discourses of psychotherapy and supervision. Thus, feminist supervision strives to subvert and interrupt the trance of powerlessness in supervisees, their clients, and ultimately the supervisor by inviting all parties to become aware of those openings where enhanced power can be observed and attained.

Within this broad aspirational construct of what constitutes interpersonal and intrapersonal power, feminist therapists invite clients to discover strategies for becoming more powerful, using the tools of psychotherapy and the relationship of therapist and client as the womb in which such power can grow. It is more usual than not for most people entering therapy to have their power be invisible and unavailable to them and to find the notion that they might have power at all frankly risible. When the feminist therapist first asks in a therapy session, "What is the powerful thing you could do now," many people's response is a variation on, "There is no powerful thing." Offering the model of power described to clients and framing power as being a continuous variable, rather than a matter of having or not having, breaks the trance of powerlessness as people begin to understand that they have already been powerful innumerable times and in a wide range of ways.

Two Sides of Power and Powerlessness
for Supervisees in Feminist Practice

Supervisees in feminist therapy are in a unique position, which the supervisor must be able to identify and appreciate. A trainee in psychology is in a position of relative powerlessness in her or his life. She or he is participating in a training process in which the message to students is that they are not as competent in the realm of human behavior as they believed coming into their graduate training. Graduate training in psychology and other helping professions is a process that is often shaming, deskilling, and undermining of the student's sense of personal power and agency, if one is to credit the personal accounts of many graduate students who have crossed my path in the four decades since my own experiences in training. In rare (although becoming more common) instances, feminists control the norms of a training program (see Gentile et al., 2009, for a description of such a program) or a particular training setting, such as a counseling center, and infuse it with empowerment and social justice norms. However, the usual scenario is that trainees enter feminist supervision more disempowered (or as my trainees would say, "jerked around") by the context of their education than otherwise.

Thus, the trainee frequently enters her or his practicum or internship training site feeling disempowered and one down in relationship to anyone in a position of authority. Yet the moment that the trainee enters the role of psychotherapist or psychological evaluator, he or she becomes the more powerful person in the interaction vis-à-vis the client. She or he then returns to supervision, in which the trainee has considerably less formal power, yet in the feminist context, is possibly more empowered than elsewhere in the training world.

A feminist supervisor must be able to hold the often confusing realities of these multiple levels of role power for the trainee firmly in mind and make them visible and explicit for the trainee. Supervision must affirm the trainee's power in her or his professional role in relationship to clients and also explore how difficult it can be for the trainee, who generally does not feel powerful, to acknowledge that she or he is, in fact, the person with greater power in her or his newly emerging professional role and identity. The feminist supervisor also can mentor trainees to explore effective means by which to become more empowered in their educational settings, offering suggestions for strategies that might raise consciousness among their program faculty or increase solidarity and collective action among students who share concerns for social justice. Sometimes the feminist supervisor can simply validate the realities that affect trainees in their interactions with other-than-liberatory educational systems.

Trainees being supervised in a feminist context have commented that this experience is disruptive to the coping strategies they have been using to survive graduate education, such as denial, compliance, and self-deprecation (Pape, 2010). A feminist supervisor has a responsibility to teach trainees how to handle this disruption in ways that will not endanger their standings in programs in which disempowerment, rigid hierarchy, and institutional betrayal often are common aspects of daily experience. Mentoring trainees in effective collective strategies for resisting the trance of misery that often is the norm in graduate training can be a gratifying aspect of being a feminist supervisor. Encouraging trainees to use their own experiences of disempowerment to deepen empathy with clients' strategies for coping in exponentially more disempowering environments, noting how psychotherapists can learn from our clients about coping in difficult or intolerable circumstances, and exposing parallel processes of learning to become empowered are components of a feminist perspective in supervision.[1]

---

[1] Some ideas in this chapter first appeared in Brown, 2010.

2

Epistemologies and Methodologies of Feminist Supervision

This chapter extends the previous examination of the core dynamics of feminist therapy practice and considers how those norms are applicable to supervision. I review the proposals of several expert authors on the topic of feminist supervision for direction as to how to deepen the feminist therapy paradigm when applied to supervision.

Szymanski's (2003, 2005) research has found that to practice feminist supervision, a supervisor must first fully comprehend and integrate feminist values and norms of practice. Feminist practice, including feminist supervision, attempts to achieve its goals through the development of an egalitarian balance of power in all relationships (Ballou, Hill, & West, 2008; Brown, 1994, 2010; Enns, 2004; Worell & Remer, 2003). In the supervision context, in which a purely egalitarian model is structurally not possible because of the need to evaluate trainees, feminist supervisors do not simply

http://dx.doi.org/10.1037/14878-003
Supervision Essentials for the Feminist Psychotherapy Model of Supervision, by L. S. Brown
Copyright © 2016 by the American Psychological Association. All rights reserved.

abandon the egalitarian ideal. Instead, they explore how to be egalitarian-near in the manner in which the supervision experience is structured in each detail, explicitly extending the model to the practice of feminist supervision and consultation.

Porter and Vasquez (1997) argued for referring to feminist supervision as *covision*, emphasizing the collaborative and egalitarian-near nature of the feminist supervision process. This terminology also emphasizes and brings supervisor attention to the importance of fidelity to the feminist ethic of empowerment in the inherently unequal supervision setting (Dutton & Rave, 1990). These authors noted that simply because a situation is inherently hierarchical does not mean that the feminist practitioner is excused from engaging in empowerment strategies or from exploring means by which a more egalitarian relationship structure can be developed. Rather, the feminist supervisor creatively strives to apply the ethic of empowerment wherever possible within supervision.

SPECIFIC STRATEGIES FOR EMPOWERING SUPERVISEES

Feminist therapy empowerment strategies have been proposed by various authors (Brown, 1994, 2010; Worell & Remer, 2003) to have several effects that are at the core of the feminist practice of psychotherapy or supervision. These strategies include consciousness raising regarding the effects of oppressive systems of power and dominance in the interpersonal and intrapsychic realms, identification of internalized memes of disempowerment in all individuals involved in feminist practice, supporting recipients of services in becoming more aware of ways in which they are able to be powerful on a range of interpersonal and intrapsychic variables, and the practice of empowered modes of interaction in the context of the relationship. Analysis of power dynamics, both in the practice setting and in life, in addition to a search for ways in which a practitioner and her or his clients engage in unaware adherence to patriarchal values, permeate the work of the feminist practitioner.

In feminist supervision, these principles of empowerment were translated by Porter and Vasquez (1997) as reflecting the following supervisory stances and necessary strategies on the part of the supervisor:

- attention to issues of power;
- the development of collaborative relationships;
- reflexivity on the part of the supervisor and between supervisor and supervisee; and
- authenticity and openness on the part of the supervisor.

A feminist supervisor's first and continuing task in the service of these four goals is to set a tone in the supervisory relationship that conveys the feminist underpinnings of the enterprise. That tone is one of respect, empowerment, and collaboration in the context of a hierarchical relationship in which evaluation will occur. This can be a daunting task in that the two goals seem diametrically opposed to one another when considered in dominant cultural frameworks. However, feminist therapy constructs of what constitutes power and empowerment inform the feminist supervisor that these phenomena are a "both/and" reality and are in fact a paradigm for all aspects of the psychotherapeutic relationship. The feminist supervisor initiates a process that models this dialectic for the trainee, a tone for relationships that does not deny the realities of power imbalances and yet simultaneously commits to the empowerment of the person with less formal role power.

It is incumbent on the feminist supervisor to assess as accurately as possible the trainee's capacities and level of development and offer the quality and quantity of supervisory support that matches where the trainee is and nourishes opportunities for the trainee's growth as an individual and a psychotherapist. A careful blend of support and autonomy characterizes all good supervision; in the case of feminist supervision, autonomy is framed within the construct of how the trainee can own more power to think effectively about what is happening in treatment and have access to the full range of emotional and embodied states that will allow attunement to clients.

Feminist supervision at its best offers a trainee the opportunity to experience being in the kind of relationship with a powerful individual that the trainee wishes to be able to offer to her or his clients. That is, it models a relationship in which the focus is on empowerment and the value of the voice of the less powerful person in the room. For a therapist to comprehend how to develop an egalitarian, empowering psychotherapy relationship, she or he must have had the experience of being in an empowering supervisory relationship that is as egalitarian as feasible given the demand characteristics of a training setting.

Supervisors who are feminist must embody the experience of empowerment with their trainees and model support for the trainee's development of her or his own voice as a therapist and her or his own theoretical orientation and style of practice. This entails the willingness to experience discomfort with a trainee perspective so long as the supervisor can be certain that safe and ethical practice is occurring and to be open to learning from trainees, not simply imparting knowledge to them.

Feminist supervisors empower trainees to learn to trust their clinical judgment through modeling of good clinical choices, mentoring of the trainee in taking graduated steps toward greater degrees of autonomy, and supporting trainees when they planfully and mindfully engage in creative applications of therapeutic interventions in support of client welfare. A feminist supervisor models the centrality of the evidence-based relationship variables to the healing process by privileging relationship, even in a more didactic phase of supervision, and by modeling transparency as her or his own errors and struggles as a psychotherapist.

SPECIFIC EDUCATIONAL AND TRAINING GOALS OF FEMINIST SUPERVISION

Because supervision is about training new psychotherapists, feminist supervision has specific educational and training goals for supervisors and supervisees that are supervision-specific expressions of feminist therapy values. Natalie Porter (2009) has been the most consistent voice in the past 30 years on the topic of feminist therapy supervision and has developed the most explicit description of a paradigm for this practice. Her work is foundational to any models of feminist supervision and is must reading for anyone wishing to describe herself or himself as a feminist supervisor. Her feminist developmental model posits the following stages of supervision in feminist practice occurring in a recursive, nonstepwise fashion:

- didactic introduction of feminist perspectives in general, then applied to the supervised work in specific;
- exploration of larger social and cultural issues of power, privilege, and oppression;
- trainee self-awareness: implicit biases, privilege and disadvantage, internalized oppression and domination; and
- development of social action perspective on psychotherapy—cultural sensitivity as first, but not sufficient, step.

Didactic Introduction of Feminist Therapy Perspectives

Supervisees come to supervision with a feminist therapist with a wide range of knowledge and misinformation about feminist therapy, its heritage, and its practices. Some supervisees are actively pursuing work with a feminist supervisor; others may be nonplussed or even hostile upon learning that this is their supervisor's theoretical orientation. In rare instances, a trainee will have had access to a feminist therapy course or will have independently pursued readings on the topic. However, because feminist practice is not widely mainstreamed in graduate programs in psychology and other helping professions, it is more likely that the supervisee will have little to no knowledge of feminist practice or may even have been misinformed as to what feminist therapy is and for whom it is helpful. Feminist therapy theory is increasingly being included in general theories of psychotherapy texts to which some, but not all, graduate students are exposed. This range of information or lack thereof is also likely to be encountered when the person is voluntarily seeking postdegree supervision or consultation.

A challenge for supervisors of graduate students is to find didactic materials that will not be perceived as adding to the burden of the already large amount of material that trainees in graduate school are required to cover for the courses they are taking. My brief text (Brown, 2010) was designed to be this sort of easier introduction to the field and can be assigned to trainees and discussed in supervision sessions in the context of case material being supervised.

Feminist supervisors can also identify certain important founding articles or book chapters, such as the article by Broverman, Broverman, Clarkson, Rosenkrantz, and Vogel (1970) on sex-role stereotyping; Chesler's *Patient and Patriarch* (1970), which succinctly covers the materials expanded on in *Women and Madness*; Smith and Siegel's (1985) chapter on power; Lerman's (1983) article on feminist theories of personality; Enns's (1992) article on the integration of various streams of feminist political philosophies into feminist therapy; or Berman's (1985) chapter on relationship overlap and ethical practice for feminist therapists. Many of these can be easily accessed in electronic form or reproduced and shared with trainees as ways of inculcating them with feminist therapy constructs.

Although there is no clear standard as to what information should be didactically acquired by a supervisee, a review of the literature on feminist supervision suggests that a feminist supervisor should be prepared to educate trainees on basic feminist therapy constructs, such as development of feminist consciousness, the nature of egalitarian relationship, meanings of multiple and intersecting identities, gender role analysis, and feminist constructions of distress and disorder. The feminist supervisor uses the supervision sessions for illustrating how these phenomena manifest in the trainee and the trainee's clients. Topics to be discussed can also include the question of what defines feminism for the trainee and the supervisor and what constitutes the trainee's relationship to feminism.

In addition to this material, feminist supervisors often introduce trainees to various guidelines for working with marginalized populations. The American Psychological Association's *Guidelines for Psychological Practice With Girls and Women*; *Guidelines for Psychological Practice With Lesbian, Gay, and Bisexual Clients*; *Guidelines for Assessment and Intervention With Persons With Disabilities*; and *Guidelines on Multicultural Education, Training, Research, Practice and Organizational Change for Psychologists* are among those most directly relevant to the emphasis of feminist supervision in developing cultural competence in trainees.

At the feminist training clinic that I directed, each training year begins with didactic material on feminist therapy, reviewing core topics and directing trainees to important documents. Trainees are also given a required reading list, with the materials discussed in a weekly readings group. Weekly didactic presentations include exploration of a range of topics related to feminist practice, with focus on increasing competencies in working with various marginalized populations. This is one example of how to infuse didactic information about feminist therapy into a training setting that is feminist at its core. Where there is only one feminist supervisor, other avenues for imparting didactic information to a trainee can be considered, such as having trainees read material specific to the clients with whom they are working or advocating to bring guest speakers on feminist topics to the training setting. What is important is that the trainee be exposed to the now-robust literature available regarding what constitutes feminist practice in psychology so that it can be integrated into the trainee's work.

Exploring Feminist Identity Development as a Component of Professional Development

Use of Self-Reflection

A model of feminist identity development (Fischer, Tokar, Mergl, Good, Hill, & Blum, 2000) can be introduced as part of this didactic process as a strategy for inviting trainee's self-reflection on where they situate themselves on the continuum of feminist identity. What has been surprising to many trainees is the degree to which they find themselves having strong attachments to feminist values in the absence of a clear identification with feminism, an invisible feminist identity that may have drawn them to seek a feminist supervisor, or has led to serendipitous alignment with feminist therapy values of practice. This eye-opening contrast between values and identity provokes useful discussion and offers opportunities for trainees to observe parallel processes between this kind of conflict for themselves and similar conflict experienced by their clients.

Trainees will vary in their degree of identification with feminism and feminist therapy. Some will not think of themselves as feminist; others will have a strong identification and involvement with some aspect of feminist politics, which may or may not mirror the politics of the particular feminist supervisor. A useful exercise for encouraging self-reflexivity about feminist identity development is to ask trainees to keep journals in which they respond weekly to the instruction "Each week please write about experiences that you have in which you become aware of the themes of gender, power, and social location in daily life, and then discuss how these social/environmental phenomena affect you as a therapist, and affect clients who you're seeing." This exercise functions to raise consciousness without imposing a particular feminist viewpoint on a trainee and evokes curiosity about the values of feminism and feminist therapy. One trainee's response to this exercise, early in training, illustrates the value of overtly raising questions about feminism and feminist identity with trainees, even those who have actively sought out feminist therapy supervision or course work:

> So what does Feminism mean to me? Right now, I honestly don't know what it means to me. Right now it feels like this threatening, unknown thing that is lurking around me and making me feel uncomfortable. I feel like I have so many misconceptions about what Feminism really is and I am blinded to the truth because of that. (Sierra Swing-Kent, personal communication, 2005, cited in Brown, 2006)

This trainee's transparent expression of her doubts opened a discussion between us about whether someone whose intersectionalities of identities had always included expressions of feminist values, but who had been taught in her family's cultural context to reject the label *feminist*, could see herself as a feminist therapist. Her later public self-identification as a feminist therapist included an analysis of how her involvement with as well as rebellion against norms of conventional femininity had confused her about what it meant to be feminist—as it continue to confuse people who first meet her and assume that a stylish feminine woman wearing high heels and makeup cannot also be radical in her feminist analysis (Swing, 2007).

that are cues to behaving adaptively, these paradigms tend to treat humans not as integrated beings but as a collection of discrete parts called sex, race, social class, and so forth, with one of those nominated as the important identity variable. A trainee entering feminist supervision may expect to be asked to think only about gender; a feminist supervisor will direct attention to an integrative model of intersectionalities of identities.

Novice psychotherapists also frequently learn in nonfeminist models of multicultural practice to feel badly about themselves, especially if they are members of dominant cultural groups. In this model of teaching about cultural competence, novice therapists usually learn that their clients who come from positions of less social power or privilege do not feel safe with them or understood by them. These trainees will learn to worry about saying or doing something insensitive, which in turn generates anxiety that in turn interferes with therapists' capacities to be fully present empathically and leads to relationship ruptures.

Culturally competent practice can be an anxiety-provoking subject. Teaching ourselves and those we supervise to mindfully and compassionately observe our past and present participation in dynamics of power, privilege, and oppression and reducing anxiety for trainees as they learn to unpack these variables in their work are central to effectively meeting this goal of feminist supervision. Trainees in the helping professions often have problematic relationships with their own experiences of power and privilege. This reflects the persistent failure of multicultural training to convey information about power, privilege, and difference in ways that do not induce guilt and shame. In one of my experiences with this issue, trainees appeared at my site after a course in which the instructor conveyed to me that he had as a stated goal the induction of "White guilt" in students; this created an atmosphere in which I, as a feminist supervisor, had to begin conversations about bias and privilege from a stance of repairing the wounds of previous training experiences.

Thus, feminist supervision focuses on the precept that "we all have multiple and intersecting identities, with multiple and varying experiences of power and powerlessness, privilege and disadvantage among them." The feminist supervisor models the use of self-reflexivity regarding her or his own identities and struggles as a target of oppression, as a member of dominant groups, and as an ally, and shares her or his journeys confronting guilt and shame. She or he also invites trainees to notice and delight in the diversity of experiences of the world that derive from these intersections, noting (as I frequently do in group supervision) that being a Euro American, cisgender woman who is a baby boomer is both different from and yet similar to being a Euro American, cisgender woman who is a millennial, for instance.

In my own work training on issues of diversity and cultural competence, I use an exercise in which I describe different groups of people and ask those present to move across the room if they are members of that group—and willing to be so identified. The instructions for the exercise explicitly encourage participants to respect their own privacy boundaries and make choices about whether or how to be visible in their various group memberships if they can make the choice to be unseen.

This allows trainees to see the vast diversity among them and also opens up discussions of privilege inherent in being able to choose to not disclose—to pass—around some aspects of identity that may be stigmatized and yet invisible. This exercise models the use of disclosure, normalizes within-group differences, and makes transparent some of the dynamics of power and privilege that are operating, unseen, among a group of trainees. This, in turn, increases anxiety-free curiosity about how these dynamics of difference might be emerging in the context of the therapy relationships that are being supervised.

As an example, Colin, a Euro American, cisgender male, advanced doctoral student in his early 30s who came from an upper-middle-class background, began to work with Roger, a mid-60s, Euro American, cisgender man who had grown up middle class and had fallen into poverty because of the effects of childhood trauma on his academic and vocational functioning. Colin initially was perplexed by Roger's apparent incessant ramblings on the theme of "I could have been a contender," focusing on the one period of good enough function in his life during his late teens. Colin felt alienated from his client and found himself falling back on strategies that he had learned in his training to try to assert control of the content of sessions, something that troubled him and which he brought to supervision for support in developing a more egalitarian response to Roger.

In supervision, I invited Colin to look at what was happening between them in terms of their diverse narratives of masculinity and the ways in which Colin might represent, to Roger, the apex of such a narrative, whereas Roger himself was defined as a failure in those terms. Colin, who despite his skills saw himself as a young, inexperienced human in contrast to Roger, was then able to look at their diverse intersectionalities of identity in the therapeutic context and see how even those aspects of identity they apparently shared were a source of shame and disempowerment for Roger. We also explored how my somewhat-invisible presence in Roger's therapy, as a Euro American, cisgender woman of Roger's generation who has had success on all of the variables with which Roger struggled, might also be evoking more shame and disempowerment for Roger, who knew, from having consented to this, that I sometimes listened to the recordings of their sessions.

This analysis of gender, power and powerlessness, generational factors, and trauma history empowered Colin to return to an egalitarian relationship with Roger. Rather than becoming distracted and at times frustrated by Roger's narrative, Colin was able to develop a more effective analysis, based in attention to Roger's intersectionalities of identities, of what might be the sources of Roger's fear of change and his apparent avoidance of what therapy had to offer. This changed perspective on Roger allowed Colin, in turn, to consider how to offer empowerment to his client from within this lens.

Colin began to explore ways to bring their shared experiences of identity as members of agent groups and the effects of those oppressive narratives on both of their lives into the relationship. His careful use of self-disclosure about his struggles with being a "real man" promoted the development, over time, of a more genuine and increasingly egalitarian relationship in which Roger finally felt sufficiently safe to be visible to and vulnerable with Colin about his tremendous fear that any attempt at change in therapy would be only another in the long list of so-called failures in his life. Feminist therapy theory codes the capacity for vulnerability as a way of being powerful in the world, and Roger was becoming, albeit tentatively, more powerful in his relationship with Colin than he had been when he had been bombastically describing the triumphs of his youth.

DEVELOPING A SOCIAL ACTION PERSPECTIVE

For a feminist practitioner, her or his psychotherapeutic work is not done when therapy ends. Rather, feminist therapy theory sees society itself as the place where pathologies fester and where interventions need to be applied. The feminist practitioner's orientation to social action does not end with strivings toward cultural competence (Brown, 2008; Comas-Díaz, 2012), and feminist supervision offers opportunities and support for trainees to develop their social action skills outside of the therapy office. This might include giving trainees in a formal setting release time counted as professional development hours for attending a psychology lobbying date, bringing up opportunities to engage in social action at demonstrations, involving trainees in doing research for or drafting amicus briefs, and exploring other forms of social justice activism. An example of this was when our clinic trainees successfully lobbied to change a state regulation that made it difficult for impoverished crime victims to fully use the victim compensation system; I coached them in meeting with the state psychological association lobbyist and went with them to the state capitol, where two of them testified at a hearing and then met with legislators.

SETTING EXPECTATIONS FOR SUPERVISION: NORMS AND EVALUATION

All supervision and consultation practice should occur within a framework of clear informed consent to participation in the process; this is not a feminist principle per se but does reflect the long-standing feminist attention to the value and necessity of informed consent for relationships between more and less powerful people in a therapeutic or therapy-near context (Hare-Mustin, Marecek, Kaplan, & Liss-Levinson, 1979). It is also a step frequently neglected in academic supervision experiences, in which a trainee chooses or is assigned to a site, then assigned to a supervisor, often with minimal input into how those relationships are formed. Chew (in press) defined the use of informed consent to feminist supervision as a supervisory "best practice," noting that trainees may not understand fully the implications of having a supervisor of a particular theoretical orientation without this kind of clear and specific consent process.

In general, graduate student trainees bring contracts from their programs that describe the formal relationship and responsibilities between a school and a training site. These contracts often make reference to the relevant ethical code governing the practice of supervisors and students and to the frequency with which formal evaluations must be submitted to the training program, but they tend to function primarily as documentation of liability rather than as any kind of trainee consent to supervision. When supervision and consultation are pursued independently outside of the graduate school framework, there are rarely norms for whether or how to formalize consent to the relationship.

What is uncommon, and from a feminist perspective very important, is the empowerment of the supervisee to fully consent to the supervision process and to know a priori the risks and benefits of supervision. This concept of "empowered consent," in which the parties clearly delineate rights and responsibilities (Brown, 1994), reflects the understandings of feminist therapy practice that every component of the relationship, beginning with the formal consent process, is one in which empowerment can and should occur.

Behavioral expectations and norms for a supervision experience should be clearly spelled out for both parties, in writing, using a framework of rights and responsibilities. For instance, a trainee should know up front how a supervisor expects the supervisee to manage the issue of risk and what consequences will ensue should a supervisee not fulfill these expectations. A supervisor should be clear about how she or he intends to supervise (in vivo, via recordings, through process discussion) and what theoretical models she or he will rely upon for understanding the trainee's work. Clear rationales for aspects of supervision should be made available; thus, at our clinic we audio-record not because that's what we do but to protect the welfare of clients and supervisees and offer additional educational time for trainees while reviewing recordings. Supervisees should be introduced to whatever forms or checklists will be used to evaluate their progress so that they can be aware from the beginning of what will be attended to by a supervisor and what dimensions will be taken into account in evaluation. A sample form from the feminist therapy training clinic that I have directed can be found in Appendix A. In addition, norms for stepwise application of remedial and disciplinary procedures should be clearly spelled out and made available to trainees at the start of the training process. An example of a supervision contract can be found in Appendix B.

All of this formal and explicit description of certain variables in the supervision functions optimally to engender trust. A supervisee should expect not to be surprised by how and on what dimensions she or he is being evaluated; nor should he or she be blindsided by a supervisor who has biases about the trainee's theoretical orientation. Supervision is inherently stressful because the supervisee makes herself or himself transparent in the service of learning and client welfare; thus, a supervisee should know what to expect and be able to rely on the informed consent process.

However, beyond the formal informed consent to supervision is the relational component of setting goals together for the supervision experience. Such a discussion should be bidirectional and occur regularly. In other words, the supervisor does not unilaterally set the expectations for feminist supervision. Instead, supervisor and supervisee develop a mutually agreed upon set of goals for *both* parties in the supervisory relationship. This makes explicit the feminist frame of mutuality and collaboration in supervision or *covision*. A feminist supervisor is not expected to be endlessly flexible with regard to the goals of supervision but should be open to some mixture of didactic and process orientation, depending upon supervisee needs and level of development. As in psychotherapy, the quality of relationship and alliance between supervisor and supervisee can make or break the quality of the learning experience. Feminist supervision, with its heavy emphasis on respect, mutuality, and empowerment in relationship, has a large investment in the development of a supervisory alliance.

INTRODUCING THE EVIDENCE BASE OF THE PSYCHOTHERAPY RELATIONSHIP

The strongest evidence base for feminist practice is that of the empirically supported psychotherapy relationship variables (Norcross, 2011). Feminist supervisors continuously find opportunities to note ways in which those relationship variables can be identified in the therapy supervised; my trainees and I joke that, like a talking doll, there seems to be a string on me that can be pulled to remind them that the relationship variables, including client and therapist contributions, account for the largest percentage of outcome variance in psychotherapy, whereas the specific intervention accounts for only 8%. Alliance, empathy, collaboration, goal consensus, positive regard, and collecting client feedback, all components of feminist practice, are among the specific psychotherapy relationship variables for which the evidence base is strong, and feminist supervision emphasizes these within the conceptual framework of client empowerment. Feminist supervision also emphasizes awareness of other variables that affect the therapy experience and assist trainees in making wise decisions about how to offer specific interventions, following Norcross's (2004) model of developing individualized client-to-treatment match. In this, feminist therapy echoes Rogers (1957, p. 11), who said, "It is the client who knows what hurts, what directions to go, what problems are crucial, what experiences are deeply buried." The construct of the "two-experts" relationship in feminist therapy is a core component of the relationship model being taught in feminist supervision.

In addition, there has been a moderate amount of research looking specifically at the application of feminist empowerment strategies, all of which underscores the importance of teaching empowerment in feminist supervision. Chandler, Worell, Johnson, Blount, and Lusk (1999) found that with both brief (four or fewer sessions) or slightly longer (seven or more sessions) therapy, clients in feminist therapy improved significantly more on empowerment variables than did those getting nonfeminist interventions and that the changes persisted at longer-term follow up. Rader and Gilbert (2005) found that self-identified feminist therapists were more likely to report engaging in power-sharing behaviors than were other therapists, a report corroborated by their clients. Niva Piran and colleagues (Oakley et al., 2013; Piran, 1999) found that clients in feminist therapy reported therapist behaviors that organized on three factors: respectful validation, empowerment, and unsilencing trauma. All three are consistent with the goal of egalitarian relationship in feminist therapy.

CONTEXT/SETTING

The setting in which supervision occurs informs how a feminist supervisor practices. This is true for any supervisor, but feminist supervisors must still contend with misinformation or even hostility on the part of trainees and sometimes colleagues, depending on the setting. In some settings (e.g., prison), the notion of client empowerment may seem to be at direct odds with the correctional nature of the context and clients' complete lack of freedom; ironically, the feminist practice question of "what is the one small thing that could empower you even a little" becomes more salient than for clients living in the free world. A feminist supervisor working in this sort of setting must explore in a sophisticated way how to adapt feminist models to work with both clients and supervisees and use the teaching opportunities offered by a hostile-to-feminism context to demonstrate how feminist principles can not only be applied but may in fact be more crucial to the good outcome of therapy than they would be in settings in which feminism is explicitly welcome.

Thus, feminist supervisors practicing in contexts informed by particular cultural, faith, or other norms and values that appear at first glance to be either nonsupportive of or inimical to feminist practice must explore, not whether to supervise there, but how to do so. Using the feminist therapy construct of empowering people to develop effective strategies for resisting oppression, the feminist supervisor can approach these challenges with a similar mind-set and then offer that to trainees.

Even in settings where feminist practice seems to find a relative welcome, as is true in many of the university and college counseling centers of the early 21st century, a feminist supervisor needs to attend to ways in which she or he can continue to deepen feminist practice and identify structural phenomena that undermine it. Directing a feminist training clinic has taught me never to take the application of feminist principles in supervision for granted and to maintain a mindful awareness of the subtle pulls to default to power-over models of interacting with a trainee.

OBSERVING THE TRAINEE IN ACTION

Feminist therapy theory is agnostic as to the most effective methodologies for documenting supervised experience. Thus, the feminist supervisor, after determining whether there are context-specific requirements, such as certain kinds of recording, should explore first the means by which she or he is most likely to be able to understand and empower the supervisees in her or his work and what model of gaining access to the supervisee's work best fits the mutual needs and theoretical models of both parties. A supervisor who is highly auditory may find it most useful not to be distracted by visual cues; a supervisor may be most informed by a review of process notes. A supervisor trained in family therapy may have viewing of videos or working behind a one-way mirror strongly integrated into her or his own practice. What is important to feminist practice is that the choice of strategy for gaining access to the work of the supervisee is one that potentially meets goals of feminist practice rather than being adopted by default.

Next, the feminist supervisor collaborates with the supervisee in developing a plan for how supervised sessions will be observed and shared with the supervisor. A discussion with clients about how their therapy sessions will be exposed in supervision must take place, with the rationale for more invasive strategies (e.g., audio or video recording) integrated into the client's goals for treatment as well as the supervisee's goals for training. Clients who are supervised must give consent for the supervision and its methodologies. In the training clinic I direct, we have had lengthy discussions with some of our clients about why we audio-record all sessions. Some clients are intensely uncomfortable with this, and trainee therapists frequently have been uncomfortable with imposing this clinic boundary and norm on clients. Feminist supervision assists the trainee and client alike to explore the requirement, not simply as a rule with which both parties must comply but as an aspect of the training process that potentially can empower both parties. Clients are offered copies of their session recordings; in one instance, the client and therapist did a ritual of destroying the recordings when the therapy relationship ended as a strategy for supporting the client's desires for privacy.

DOCUMENTATION: KEEPING RECORDS AS A FEMINIST

Teaching feminist models for documentation of psychotherapy services is an often-invisible and yet important component of feminist supervision. Psychotherapy services must be documented because the therapy chart is a legal document. Charts must be protected under relevant state and federal laws regarding privacy and confidentiality of client records. All of this seems superficially to have no relationship to specifically feminist concerns.

Yet as Luepnitz (1988) has noted, a feminist therapist "sets the fee as a feminist," and all of the business practices of feminist therapy require scrutiny so that they support feminist therapy's ultimate liberatory goals. Consequently, feminist practice enters into this aspect of supervision with questions of how the content of a chart can empower or disempower the client. A feminist model teaches "golden rule" note taking; that is, take only the kind of notes about your clients that you would feel comfortable having your own therapist write about you. Notes are analyzed in supervision for information about therapist implicit bias that might emerge in how behaviors are described. Because some jurisdictions allow clients to request that no notes be taken of their sessions, feminist supervision in those locales includes discussion of how a feminist therapist responds to such requests so as to empower the client while not disempowering the therapist or creating undue vulnerability for either party.

TAILORING SUPERVISION TO SUPERVISEE'S DEVELOPMENT, SETTINGS, AND CLIENTS

In Jewish tradition, there is the concept of the "four children": the wise child, who gobbles up knowledge; the obstinate child, who cannot see how this information has anything to do with him or her; the simple child, who is just beginning to learn; and the one who does not know how to ask. A specific teaching strategy is prescribed for each of these locations on the continuum of openness to knowledge.

Feminist supervision (and to some extent all supervision) recognizes these four stage of acquisition of skill that occur in the supervisory process. A trainee who has already read everything available about feminist practice and has benefited from prior feminist supervision is prepared for a more sophisticated discussion of the epistemologies of distress than is a student in her or his first practicum. A trainee who had no desire to have feminist supervision and finds herself or himself receiving it because of being assigned to a feminist supervisor initially may not see how feminist therapy theory has relevance for her or his theoretical orientation or practice style; that trainee requires and deserves both respect for her or his starting position and invitations to see how and where feminist and other models intersect and integrate.

Early in feminist practice, questions were raised as to whether there are clients who might not benefit from a feminist perspective. Initially, feminist therapy was developed for work with women but today is being applied to all genders and across the life-span. However, because of the emphasis on empowerment, questions continue to be raised about the appropriateness of this model for work with correctional populations. These questions stem from a somewhat narrow and unsophisticated understanding of client empowerment. Work by feminist therapists in corrections settings with both women and men has demonstrated that an empowerment perspective may be particularly well-suited for work with individuals who are both systemically rendered powerless (by being inmates or court ordered into treatment) and who have most frequently entered the legal system because of ineffective attempts to manage other experiences of disempowerment (e.g., racism, trauma exposure).

A feminist analysis conceives of criminal activities as evidence of such disempowered and ineffective strategies and in corrections populations concerns itself with supporting more effective strategies that reduce the risks of recidivism by directly addressing issues of oppression and trauma as precursors to entry into the legal system.

Feminist supervision with clients such as these invites trainees to see their clients through the feminist, rather than standard correctional, lens and to be culturally competent in the corrections setting while integrating the insights and perspectives of feminist practice. This exemplifies the feminist supervision strategy of never abandoning a feminist epistemology but rather tailoring it to meet the realities of the clients and contexts in which the feminist practitioner is operating.

INDIVIDUAL AND GROUP SUPERVISION

"Groupervision" (Gina Scarsella, personal communication, 2015), like group psychotherapy, often is attractive within a feminist model because of the opportunities it offers for trainee empowerment, similar to the ways in which clients can be empowered by what occurs in a therapy group. In group supervision, the power of the supervisee can be modulated by the power of peers in the group to offer consultation to one another adjunctive to the supervisor's comments. Consciousness raising about the vicissitudes of the work of a psychotherapist occurs most effectively in a group setting, where trainees are exposed to one another's challenges and triumphs and are able to normalize one another's experiences in manners that are far more empowering than when reassurances come from a supervisor. Groups in which there are members of more than one gender present also provide rich opportunities for in vivo exploration of the effects of gender dynamics and the nonaware expressions of privilege or compliance that can be detected when the group is mixed sex.

However, group supervision is not a prescribed feminist model, and anecdotal evidence suggests that most feminist supervision occurs in dyads. Because the potential for aggravation of systemic power differentials is increased in individual supervision settings, a feminist supervisor takes extra time and care to explore, both at the onset of the supervisory relationship and then throughout the process, how dynamics of power differentials, identities, and privilege are affecting, for good or ill, the supervisory process.

Supervisee preferences for individual or group supervision are taken into account to the greatest degree possible. For example, a supervisee who knows herself or himself to be introverted and have difficulties speaking up or being transparent in a group can be mentored into becoming more able to function with comfort in a wider range of settings while also being supported in individual supervision time. However, because supervisees generally are not offered choice regarding how they will be supervised, it is incumbent on the feminist supervisor to consider how to structure the supervision so that it remains true to feminist principles of egalitarianism and includes analyses of gender and power.

CONCLUSION

So what does this all look like when put into practice? In Chapter 3, I explore and analyze a particular supervision/consultation session and demonstrate how feminist principles inform what happens. Chapter 3, like the DVD *Feminist Therapy Supervision* from which the discussion is derived, demonstrates how the general principles of feminist supervision practice are applied in vivo.

3

Structure and Process
of Feminist Supervision

SETTING THE FRAME

Supervision in feminist practice is structured in a manner similar to that of other forms of feminist practice. That is, it begins with a collaboratively developed framework for the focus of an ongoing supervisory relationship, which is revisited during any given supervisory encounter. As noted elsewhere in this volume, a feminist supervision relationship begins with a clear agreement, preferably in writing, in which parameters of the process are made clear. When supervision is occurring in an evaluative setting in which there are knowable consequences for identified problematic behaviors, the nature of those behaviors and the specifics of the consequences should be clearly explained. The specific standards by which a supervisee is being measured should never be in doubt. Systemic strategies for empowerment, reducing shame, and increasing the likelihood of mutual vulnerability are all inherent in these opening moves.

http://dx.doi.org/10.1037/14878-004
Supervision Essentials for the Feminist Psychotherapy Model of Supervision, by L. S. Brown

In addition, a feminist supervisory relationship should begin with, and continue to address, the question of what the supervised person's goals are. Supervisor and supervisee should collaborate on goals, with increasing weight given to the supervisee's desires as she or he matures in practice. A feminist supervisor resists any urges to simply tell a trainee what to do. Instead, she or he collaborates on goals, meeting the trainee where she or he is developmentally. This introduces the supervisee to the egalitarian framework of the relationship.

For example, a trainee in her or his initial clinical experience may or may not have a clear idea of what her or his personal and professional goals are, or the trainee may have an unrealistic set of expectations about what she or he can accomplish early in training. The supervisory task is to empower the trainee to be able to reflect effectively on how to determine tasks for the learning experience that derive from her or his own values, experiences, and long-term professional hopes and objectives while actively including the supervisor's wisdom and perspective in the mutual goal-setting process. Even when a trainee is not well prepared to collaborate, feminist supervision keeps its commitment to collaboration and empowerment, modeling this set of egalitarian strategies from the first.

DEVELOPMENTALLY INFORMED EMPOWERMENT

The trainee who says, "I don't know, you tell me," is encouraged to see her or his experience of not being able to find her or his voice as parallel process to that of clients, and the supervisor models the use of inductive methodologies to assist the trainee in identifying goals, illustrating along the way how the trainee therapist can use this methodology with similarly uncertain clients. Modeling empowerment methodologies begins with the first exchanges between supervisor and supervisee and continues throughout the relationship.

Conversely, a trainee who is further in professional development, such as the supervisee in the video who is seeking consultation after licensure, may have a clear and well-defined set of desires regarding the supervision process. This does not silence the feminist supervisor; in this example, the collaboration occurs with the supervised person taking the lead, and the supervisor perhaps reserving input until after she or he has had the opportunity to better know this person's practice.

In the session shown in the DVD *Feminist Therapy Supervision*, you can see what happens in a feminist supervisory relationship that has developed over a period of 13 years. Although there continues to be a large difference between us in terms of clinical experience, I am clear that I respect her capacities as an early career psychologist and am able to see the growth and development she has manifested in that time. Simply because I am identified as more expert, I do not assume that I am the only person with useful knowledge in the relationship. This is not only because my supervisee is currently at this more advanced level of skill. My treating her inherent capacities and extant knowledge with respect has been part of our relationship from the first, during the time that she was a graduate student and more of a beginner. The power differential, which once was stark, has grown nearly undetectable over the course of time. Samantha, my supervisee, has developed trust in my intentions when I challenge her; she has also developed a willingness to challenge me and to weigh her own perceptions against my feedback. Thus, I encourage her to argue with my interpretation of what I am hearing. This is an intentional feminist maneuver that aims to actively encourage supervisees to rely upon their own authority and not to simply comply with a supervisor even when they believe that person to be in error. This is not a knee-jerk avoidance of authority on the part of the supervisor. Rather, it is an active engagement in collaboration with supervisees and a strategy for empowering them to disagree assertively, rather than comply and resist in an indirect manner.

This egalitarian connection between us started with our first supervisory experience, when I gently confronted her about the quality of her work and let her know that I could see that she was not showing me everything of which she was capable. In other words, I started by reflecting her competence to her as a way of framing the problems in the work she was submitting. Frequently, trainees earlier in development situate on two poles: overly confident or overly cautious. These positions often are informed by gender, culture of origin, social class background, and other identity dynamics that have an impact on people's sense of entitlement. Samantha's first supervised material was exemplary of those factors. She held back at first, not trusting that I, as the professor and person in position of authority, would want to see her demonstrating the best of her capacities or challenging me in any way. On the contrary, when working with new trainees who have a larger loading of privilege in their identity intersectionalities, I have found that the role of the supervisor is to empower such trainees to embrace their novice status rather than attempt a show of bravado. Or, as is shown in the DVD, I empower trainees to relieve themselves of perfectionistic standards of performance and instead adopt a stance of planning to do their work as well as possible at each moment as a therapist.

What is important in all of this is that there is a collaborative and clear agreement creating the frame for the supervisory relationship. Similar to the frame in psychotherapy, the frame in feminist supervision delineates norms and boundaries. One of these important norms and boundaries, which has been touched on throughout this book, has to do with the matter of whether and to what degree the supervised person will be asked to disclose personal details when and if the supervision touches on problematic countertransference dynamics.

USES OF SELF-DISCLOSURE: SUPERVISEE AND SUPERVISOR

Supervisee Use of Self-Disclosure

The companion DVD to this book specifically illustrates the use of this empowerment strategy, which has already been referred to in this text. Because of our long history of working together, Samantha has disclosed to me over time many of the personal details that inform her countertransferences with clients, including some of the specific countertransference dynamics that are the focus of our work in the recorded session. This session is the third or fourth of these discussions of struggles with countertransference that we have been having over the year preceding the recording of the DVD, and the reference to her personal history as it became relevant to her problems with countertransference occurs in the context of those earlier discussions; thus, when supervisees disclose personal material, it is both a consensual and a gradual process in which the supervisee's comfort with being more translucent is allowed to develop at her or his pace, not that of the supervisor. These disclosures were always made at her initiation, and she controlled the timing and amount of detail she shared with me. When supervising her or consulting with her on her work, I would ask, as I often do when noticing a pattern in a supervisee's difficulties across clients, whether she was aware of personal dynamics that might be informing her stuck places. I also would make clear that she was free to determine when or if she would answer that question.

Samantha, as is true for anyone who I supervise, determined where to set her privacy boundary on every occasion. There was never a point at which I tried to argue to her that such disclosures were mandatory, nor did a higher level of disclosure at one point foreclose less disclosure at a later point. Feminist supervisors respect trainees' right to say no after they have said yes. When she did disclose personal material, we spent time processing together what it meant for her to allow me closer into her core.

Supervisor Use of Self-Disclosure

Almost always, these occasions also included some enhanced level of parallel self-disclosure on my part. This is an intentional empowerment tool, used with the goal of rebalancing power and moving toward more egalitarian dynamics at those moments when trainees may feel most vulnerable and power-down. In many instances, I would notice a dynamic in myself parallel to those she was consulting on and disclose about that in advance of asking her for any disclosure of her own personal material. A component of feminist and egalitarian supervision involves the supervisor reflecting, for the benefit of the trainee, about her or his own experiences tripping over unexplored personal territories in the context of treatment and being willing to initiate taking the risk to discuss blunders rather than waiting for the trainee to be the first to disclose difficulties. A feminist supervisor knows that some of the best teaching happens through sharing one's errors and confusion because these create egalitarian teachable moments.

I have repeatedly, over time, let Samantha know that if she wanted to share such information, I would be honored to hear it, and that if she chose not to, I would respect her privacy boundaries and her judgment regarding what to share at each step of the way. This both/and approach to the sharing of personal information is important in a feminist model; the trainee controls the information flow, and the supervisor creates a framework in which that information can be safely contained if and when it is shared.

I KNOW YOU KNOW: TITRATING SUPERVISEE VULNERABILITY

Early in the discussion in the DVD, I tell Samantha that it sounds as if she is encountering dynamics in her relationships with certain clients that refer to pieces of her personal history. We were both conscious of the unique context in which this discussion of her countertransference was occurring (e.g., a DVD that might be seen by thousands of people with whom she is not acquainted and who need not know the specifics regarding the source of this countertransference piece). We had discussed, in supervision sessions prior to recording the one on the DVD, some of the countertransference dynamics that eventually emerged in the recorded discussion and decided in advance where to set her privacy boundaries. We mutually protected her privacy boundaries in that exchange.

Trainees often begin their work with a feminist supervisor after having been in a setting in which there is no such respect for trainee privacy. Some supervisees have described being coerced into disclosure of personal information on various specious grounds (e.g., "How can you ask your clients to share this kind of information with you if you can't share it with me?"). The answer is: "You are not my therapist; you are my supervisor who is evaluating me." This is indeed a difficult thing to say to the person doing the evaluating! These trainees believe, incorrectly, that they must spontaneously share private personal information in supervision. The feminist supervisor's job is to preempt this violation of a trainee's boundaries by establishing as early as possible the notion of respect for privacy and the trainee's rights to make decisions about what will and will not be shared. Trainees working in psychodynamic models who have been in psychoanalytic supervision, which is more closely akin to psycho-analytic psychotherapy, may be at particular risk from this kind of belief system, but this system is not limited to this group of trainees. As noted many times in this book, a feminist supervisor understands that shame is a disempowering experience and initiates the norm of not intentionally inducing shame in trainees with an early-on discussion about the trainee's right to define the parameters of what and how he or she will share personal life information.

As discussed elsewhere in this book, even in instances in which there is concern for a trainee's possible impairment, a feminist supervisor is careful to balance the welfare and protection of clients against the welfare and protection of trainees. Thus, a feminist supervisor seeks only that personal information from a trainee that is pertinent to training goals and to the welfare of all involved parties, and requests information about a trainee's therapy only when client welfare is clearly at risk.

GOAL SETTING

Encounter Goals

After establishing an overarching agreement about the goals of supervision, a feminist supervisor initiates each contact by questioning the supervisee as to her or his particular goals for that encounter. "What do you want me to listen/watch for" is a common question occurring before a supervisee plays a recording of a session. This does not stop the supervisor from also attending to other matters that emerge, but the trainee in feminist supervision is empowered to become a better observer of her or his own work by having the responsibility, when possible, to determine the focus for a supervision session. This is a strategy in which the trainee becomes empowered to see herself or himself as capable of analyzing and thinking critically about her or his own work, and it deepens the capacities of the therapist's observing ego, which is so essential to ongoing practice over time.

In the companion DVD, I begin with this question, and follow the direction set by Samantha in that first encounter. She wanted to become less "stuck" with those clients with whom she was experiencing a certain kind of avoidant countertransference and to be able to feel safe and capable of demonstrating therapeutic vulnerability with such clients for whom she currently felt emotionally defended and not as present as she would like. The directions that I, as the supervisor, took in responding to this set of goals reflected my understandings of what she asked for. At different points during the session, we notice together her approach to and avoidance of the topic and the parallel process occurring between her psychotherapy work and our supervision experience. Had I, at any point, wished to expand the parameters of the process, I would have asked and collaborated with her in doing so. Similarly, she was free throughout to modify the direction of the supervision should it become apparent to her that a different course would be more fruitful and helpful to her.

Leading by Following

As a feminist supervisor, I do not attempt to impose a structure a priori on a supervision session. Instead, I lead by following. The supervised person has a direction in which he or she initially wishes to go. The supervisory tasks then become those of following closely, listening carefully, and inquiring of oneself, "How do I empower this person to become the therapist we both know she or he can be?"

DIFFICULT DIALOGUES AND DIFFERENCE

Interwoven into the fabric of feminist supervision are continuing dialogues, sometimes difficult, about identities, culture, and the effects of the intersectional identities of therapist, client, and supervisor on the therapeutic process. A feminist supervisor must be engaged in her or his own work on deepening cultural competence and should be familiar with emerging models for understanding identity development that move away from earlier stage models and instead address integratively the experiences brought to therapy and supervision because of the multiplicity of identities present.

It is typical for a feminist supervisor to invite trainees to reflect on how these various identity variables are informing not only the therapeutic relationship and its dynamics but also the nature of the client's distress, the sources of clients' resilience and capacities, and the trainee's understandings of her or his role in the therapeutic relationship. Thus, in the companion video I pay close attention to when Samantha does and does not allude to clients' gender, age, or other identity characteristics. I query her directly as to whether some aspect of socially constructed identity variables might play a part in her struggles with being emotionally available to or establishing boundaries with certain clients. On reflection, she comes to the conclusion that this is not likely the case, but a feminist supervisor will remain open to listening for these possibilities and raising them directly with a trainee.

This discussion was not simply about the nonconscious dynamics between client and therapist. It was, as it should be in feminist supervision, an exploration of sophisticated understandings of the many ways in which people's intersectional identities express themselves in the therapeutic encounter.

INVITING TRAINEES TO VALUE CULTURAL COMPETENCE IN PRACTICE

Not all trainees will be as sophisticated in their understandings of cultural competence or as committed to its centrality to their practice as is Samantha. It is unusual for a trainee who actively seeks a feminist supervisor to be resistant to integrating cultural competence into supervision. However, in some instances a trainee is assigned to a feminist supervisor for reasons other than her/his feminist practice, perhaps because of other special skills the supervisor holds. Or a trainee may simply be assigned to the supervisor available at a particular practicum or internship site, and thus cross the path of a feminist supervisor. Such trainees may not yet understand how culturally competent practice is foundational to excellence in the application of all psychotherapeutic interventions. They may object to the supervisor's perspective that in order to effectively apply the thing for which they are officially getting supervision (be it cognitive–behavioral therapy, acceptance and commitment therapy, eye movement desensitization and reprocessing, relational psychoanalysis, or any other form of psychotherapy), they should consider the work in the context of therapist's, client's, and supervisor's intersectionalities of identity.

Because culturally competent practice produces the sort of evidence-based therapist behaviors that account for significant percentages of the variance for good outcomes in psychotherapy (Duncan, Miller, & Wampold, 2009; Norcross, 2011), feminist supervisors having difficult dialogues with trainees about cultural competence have a powerful opportunity to educate trainees about the general research literature on psychotherapy relationships and the specifics of how those findings inform the necessity of embracing a culturally competent perspective. The empowerment challenge to the trainee is to invite trainees to consider how they might unintentionally undercut their capacities as therapists by ignoring this information. The empowerment challenge to the supervisor is to invite trainees to see the salience of cultural competence to their work in a manner that is not threatening to the trainee's sense of self as a person of goodwill or shaming around their devaluation of the topic.

This topic presents excellent opportunities for the feminist supervisor to use transparency and self-disclosure about her or his own experiences of learning to value cultural competence. For trainees whose identities are primarily those of agent group membership, these can be conversations requiring much supervisory skill so that trainees are not shamed by their developmental levels with regard to this topic.

EMPOWERMENT: KEEPING OUR EYES ON THE PRIZE

Balancing Insights

Throughout all of this, an overarching goal of supervision is empowerment of the supervisee, a point that bears repeating simply because it is so central to feminist supervisory models. The trainees I supervise will become my colleagues in due time. They will need epistemologies of feminist practice on which they can rely during the thousands of future hours in which they sit, alone, with clients.

A feminist supervisor thus must balance offering insights to a trainee with evoking them from trainees themselves. Simply because one, as a supervisor, thinks one has a clear notion of what is making a therapy difficult for a trainee does not mean that one should share that information as the first supervisory intervention. Socratic questioning is a foundational tool for feminist supervisory practice because it inherently assumes that the capacity to know that answer lies as much in trainees as in the supervisor asking the questions. Empowering trainees to develop their skills for understanding what is happening in their work means that they will be increasingly able to come to supervision sessions with an already well-developed set of hypotheses about what has happened and more erudite questions about how next to proceed.

Feminist supervisors can also be less sophisticated and knowledgeable about an aspect of cultural competence than a particular trainee. In the egalitarian supervisory relationship of feminist practice, the supervisor models the welcome of consciousness raising about her or his own area of growth and actively values the wisdom and contributions of the trainee. For example, I have deepened palpably in my understandings of social class and immigration experiences because of my relationships with trainees who have felt safe enough to challenge my areas of privileged unawareness. I do not rely on my trainees to do this for me; rather, the nature of the feminist supervisory relationship and the reciprocity embedded in the egalitarian relationship has allowed them to feel safely empowered to point out to me those places where I had been stepping on their toes inadvertently.

Trainees Working With High-Risk Clients

Empowering trainees takes on special meaning when a client is engaging in risky and dangerous behaviors or is threatening harm to self or others. One of the most helpless experiences that therapists have is in working with people who are wrestling with decisions about death and life or who appear to be on a self-destructive course even when death is not the specific goal. Suicidal, violent, and self-destructive behaviors are among those most likely to deskill a therapist, no matter how experienced. These actions in a client evoke fear, anxiety, and feelings of helplessness and hopelessness in therapists, no matter how experienced the therapist. When these behaviors are occurring in the clients being seen by one's trainee, the urge may come upon even the most feminist of supervisors to drop the egalitarian stance and simply take over so as to protect everyone, including themselves, from the client's risky actions.

Ironically, this is the time when the collaborative and empowering nature of feminist supervision may be *most* necessary. The client engaging in risky behaviors or contemplating suicide or violence against others often is experiencing depths of disempowerment that are being responded to with powerfully ineffective self-soothing techniques. Yet this vision of at-risk clients constructs them as attempting to solve the problems of extreme powerlessness: in other words, searching for empowerment by the only means they know or to which they have current access.

The feminist supervisor offers this construct to trainees dealing with at-risk clients, inviting the trainee to feel empowered by developing a conceptual framework for making sense of what appears to be dangerous and frightening behavior. The supervisor can model therapist empowerment by discussing self-soothing and self-care strategies for therapists in these kinds of high-anxiety situations and supporting trainees in using those skills. The egalitarian supervisory relationship becomes cast as a team working together to keep the client as safe as possible and the trainee not traumatized by the risky behaviors to which she or he is witness. Feminist supervisors can offer models for working with at-risk clients that eschew controlling strategies when possible in favor of those empowering the client and can model the use of decision-making paradigms that balance client safety and client autonomy. Assisting trainees to work with clients so as to differentiate times when the client needs the therapist to substitute her or his judgment for the client's from those when the therapist is simply anxious about the client's judgment are especially helpful; as I often say to trainees, becoming a therapy client does not mean giving up the right to do stupid and risky things. It means agreeing to discuss those things and their meanings and motivations with one's therapist.

The feminist supervisor can emphasize the value of empowering oneself as a therapist so that it becomes possible to make the most effective decisions with and for an at-risk client, demonstrating that even in the most difficult of therapeutic circumstances the goal of empowerment need not be set entirely aside.

Thus, at each step of a feminist supervisory relationship, the questions of how to empower the trainee and her or his clients, how to inculcate feminist analysis of gender and power, and how to integrate culturally competent perspectives into the treatment will be detectable. The process of feminist supervision is one in which all of these principles are embodied, overtly or more subtly.

The take-home message from all of this is that feminist supervision is a creative engagement with the question "How do I empower the trainee?" The answers to this are as many and varied as the people supervised and the clients they treat. These answers also may change when, as I discuss next, problems occur in the supervisory relationship.

4

Handling Common Supervisory Challenges

The feminist model of covision assumes there will be a reciprocal process between supervisor and supervisee such that each grows as a therapist and a feminist during their work together. No matter what theory of supervision is embraced, a supervisor will encounter the full range of behaviors in those she or he supervises. Most supervisory experiences are a delight in which the supervisor's own practice is enriched by the process and the supervisee grows in her or his capacity to be an effective and compassionate psychotherapist.

However, there are times that supervisees or particular supervisor/ supervisee relationships present challenges, some of which are common to all psychotherapy supervision and others of which derive in part from feminist principles of relationship that create tensions within a context of necessary hierarchy. As I tell the trainees who staff the feminist therapy clinic I direct, we have a horizontal structure except when it comes to issues of risk

http://dx.doi.org/10.1037/14878-005
Supervision Essentials for the Feminist Psychotherapy Model of Supervision, by L. S. Brown

to our clients or remediation for a trainee. At those junctures, I must own the responsibility and the power that goes with it for the protection and well-being of all involved. Feminist supervision practice focuses on how to empower the parties involved when these challenges arise. Ironically, the goal of empowerment may be difficult to achieve in some difficult supervision relationships when the goals of the supervisor and the supervisee are at serious cross purposes.

DEALING WITH "DIFFICULT" SUPERVISEES

As noted earlier, feminist practice perceives graduate training in professional psychology and other mental health fields as frequently constituting a trauma reenactment on the part of faculty and supervisors. Based on the stories told by countless trainees and colleagues, both during my own training and in the four decades since, it would seem that many of those currently in positions of authority vis-à-vis trainees were themselves the recipients of the worst possible supervision experiences. They were shamed and disempowered by those who trained and supervised them, and they in turn shame and disempower the ones they train, having internalized dysfunctional models of how to educate more junior therapists. One consequence of this pattern of reenacting shaming, and thus potentially traumatizing, supervisory experiences, has been that it is common for supervisees to enter the supervision dyad with the expectation that the latest supervisor will engage in such a reenactment. Dynamics that resemble transference begin to color the supervisory relationship and can lead to impasses in supervision not dissimilar to those that occur in psychotherapy.

I sense that some unknown percentage of "difficult" supervisees are not fundamentally hard to supervise or difficult as human beings in some characterological way. Rather, it is that the supervisee so expects to be shamed and humiliated in supervision that she or he engages in behaviors that invite the supervisor into yet another reenactment in which both parties misperceive the motivations and intentions of the other. If the trainee is also dealing with other dynamics of shame and disempowerment stemming from aspects of personal life history, such as target group identities or personal experiences of trauma, the challenge for the feminist supervisor is to remain in teaching mode while at the same time noting, in the most empowering manner possible, that these are matters that would benefit from being addressed therapeutically. The following case example illustrates this phenomenon.

Carly was a working-class, Euro American woman, the first in her family to attend college, with a personal history of childhood trauma for which she had not sought treatment because of financial constraints. A student in a doctor of psychology (PsyD) program, she worked as a residential counselor in a group home for adults with developmental disabilities, where she was paid minimum wage, juggling that job with raising her 8-year-old son as a single parent and attending classes in her doctoral program in the evenings and on weekends. Graduate school had been repeatedly shaming for her. Although intellectually capable, Carly's education before graduate school had not prepared her to write scholarly papers, and her work had taught her skills that were directly opposite the ones she was expected to demonstrate in her counseling classes and practica. She felt marginal as a student, frequently comparing herself to her more privileged peers, and had been on the receiving end of harsh critiques from many members of her program's faculty because the realities of her life meant that she often had to ask for extensions on due dates.

She came to practicum at my training site because she was drawn to its emphasis on feminist, multicultural trauma practice. As we learned together later in the year, she nonetheless unconsciously expected to experience the same kinds of shaming and rigid hierarchical structures that had predominated her learning experiences until that time. She was, as she shared with me later, rendered uncomfortable by the message that our clinic was one in which we engaged in shared decision making and where the power hierarchy was as flat as possible. "You were still the one evaluating me," she told me, "And so none of that verbiage mattered to me. I didn't believe that I had any power." I, too naively, had the belief that by simply enunciating and practicing feminist principles of empowerment and modeling egalitarian relationships even while acknowledging the reality of the evaluative hierarchy in which the training was occurring, I would be credible to trainees and earn their trust. There was also the matter of our social class differences. I was raised in the middle class, am visibly financially secure today, and have never been a parent. Carly knew that I had no real understanding of her life and made the assumption that I would judge her for it, as had so many other people of my class background.

As a result of these unspoken expectations, supervision with Carly initially was frustrating for both of us. Although I often gave her positive feedback because she was a gifted and creative therapist who worked well with our challenging client population, she appeared to ignore or brush that off and to fixate on and feel shamed by any suggestions I made about how she could do something differently or more effectively. She frequently would become teary when flooded with shame and excuse herself from group supervision to compose herself. This created disruption in the supervision group because other trainees were at a loss as to how to make sense of her behaviors. She began to come late to supervision and to be out ill too many times on supervision days.

After this had been going on for 2 months, I asked her to meet with me individually to look at the process of what was occurring between us. I carefully and specifically framed this meeting not as remediation or disciplinary but rather as an attempt to break through the distressing dynamic that was characterizing our relationship. I also framed it as looking at *both* of our parts in what was happening, rather than as an examination of her errors or problems alone. This explicit framing of the supervision problem as not hers alone but rather *ours*, and a relational phenomenon, set the stage for what happened next.

At the meeting she took the risk of disclosing her expectations of me—that I was likely being disingenuous about being egalitarian and, like other authority figures in her training, was mainly interested in protecting myself and my license from her missteps as a trainee. She had arrived at our meeting expecting me to have lied to her about its purpose and was bristling, prepared to cite chapter and verse from the clinic's policy handbook about why I could not fire her from the placement—which, of course, was completely opposite my intentions.

My genuine shock and surprise at her expectations, as well as my transparent distress on her behalf, began to change the trajectory of our interaction. In turn, she was surprised by my transparency and shocked into seeing me as a human being, not as some generic powerful authority figure. Once we had broken through the collective trance of powerlessness, we were able to explore some of the dynamics of power and privilege that were making her experience of working with me (or as she then insisted on saying, "under you, Laura,") frightening for her: my role power, my age, my status in the profession, and my class background, all of which were factors that she did not have the tools with which to deal effectively. Similarly, my admiration for her capacities and my genuine sense of her as a highly competent junior colleague had allowed me to distract myself from the ways in which none of that mattered where her core beliefs about the training setting were concerned. As the meeting progressed, Carly allowed herself to risk being more transparent about the experiences that had led her to expect that I would betray her as well as my stated principles. Betrayal of trust had played a prominent role in her narrative; as I stated, there was no reason for her to expect anything different from me, even though she was hoping for it.

I proposed that we collaborate on changing her narratives about herself and me and the training process at our clinic. I told her that I wasn't interested in continuing to be part of her reenactment, and that since I had become a part of it, I was invested in us disrupting that narrative and finding a new and more empowering one for her. I asked her to pay attention to the experiences of her peers at the training site, noting that she was not the only "first to college" or the only person with a childhood trauma history among the training group that year (or among her supervisors, something of which she was only peripherally aware until that meeting). Applying feminist principles of empowerment, I asked Carly what I, as a supervisor, and the organization, as a feminist clinic, could do to empower her to view herself in a new way as a clinician. We agreed that rather than her leaving supervision every time she felt awash in shame that she would use some of the grounding skills that she was successfully teaching to her clients to remain in the room, notice what was actually happening, and disrupt her inner narrative about her worthlessness. She asked me to slow her down when she was receiving positive feedback so that she could take it in.

We also discussed the issue of parallel process between Carly and her clients. I asked her what she could learn from them about disruption of narratives of powerlessness and what she was learning from them about how her power in role interfered with that process in their relationships. She told me that this was the first time that she had finally "gotten it" about the issue of the parallels between ourselves as therapists/humans and our clients; before, she said, she had simply thought that I was trying to shame her even more by noticing how like her clients she was. We spent time exploring how difficult it was for her to empower her clients through the strategy of seeing their common humanities and struggles and discussed the "there but for fortune" theme of her work with people who "look like my family members." Her sense of being an impostor sitting on the therapist side of the interaction and the effect of this impostor experience on how she received supervisory feedback also became more apparent and knowable for both of us as having created some of her difficulties in internalizing positive supervisory feedback.

This intervention proved to be successful from the perspective of all parties involved. Carly became more able to receive feedback of both kinds. When offered opportunities for leadership roles among her peers, she reflected more carefully on whether taking them would undermine her precariously balanced life of classes, work, and parenting, which had been her pattern in the past, or whether that role fit well in her personal and career needs. She worked less hard to prove either her worth or her worthlessness to me. Once she was out of shame mode, she was able to ask me for referrals to different low-fee psychotherapy clinics where her identity as a psychotherapist would not become an obstacle to good care. She became more able to be in the room with her clients in an empowering manner. Our relationship blossomed into one of active mentorship and, over the course of several years, friendly colleagues.

Oppositional Responses

Not all problematic trainees will respond well to feminist interventions. This is particularly the case when a trainee is struggling with issues of impairment or when there appear to be rigid character structures that undermine the strategy of empowerment.

Lissa, an upper-middle-class, mixed-heritage woman who identified as Asian American, had glowing letters of recommendation from other supervisors and faculty at her graduate program and had performed well at her interview for a position as an intern at our training site. It was a surprise to me and her individual supervisor to encounter someone who could not have been more different in her behaviors and attitudes from the woman described in those letters or who appeared at the interview. Once she started work, she presented a combination of oppositional reactions to supervisors combined with unusually high levels of dependency on them for emotional support and reassurance. She appeared to tolerate her clients' needs and emotions poorly. Although she knew that our clinic specialized in treating trauma survivors and had been told that chronic suicidality was a common problem with which our clients struggled, she expressed anger at having to deal with clients' suicidal feelings and having to be available for the implementation of their safety plans. She frequently came to supervision unprepared and repeatedly expressed that her main emotion in relationship to clients was frustration, reporting that she felt rejected by them when they did not respond to her interventions. She had a high client drop-out rate, and two clients called me to voice concerns about the care she was giving them.

My assistant director and I asked Lissa to meet with us to discuss ways we could support her in becoming more autonomous and more effective with her clients. We decided to utilize a strategy that had been effective with other trainees who had found themselves struggling and offered her additional supervision time with an experienced colleague. My colleague and I were dumbfounded when Lissa declared this offer "punitive and infantilizing" and refused it.

I told her that her stance seemed in direct contrast to her frequently expressed needs for additional time with her supervisors. Because I knew she was struggling, I had not wanted to formally remediate but given the nature of her response to our informal offers of assistance, I would need to develop a formal remediation plan so that we could empower her to succeed in her internship. The emphasis of the discussion was on how we could collectively make the experience one in which Lissa experienced herself as competent and emotionally well-regulated in her work, a stance that I saw as an empowering one. Both my assistant and I attempted to normalize some of her struggles as a means of reducing shame for her.

Lissa was withdrawn and communicated little during the remainder of the meeting, despite repeated attempts by both my assistant director and me to draw her into being an active part of the decision-making process. A week later, she asked for a meeting with me at which she announced that she was resigning from her internship because she had decided that I did not like her and that I was "out to get" her. She implied that my alleged animus was racist in its origins. I was in shock. I spent the remainder of the time attempting a repair with her, still unsure of how I had ruptured the relationship, although quite willing to accept the hypothesis that I had indeed done something serious enough for her to sacrifice an internship and have to start the entire process of application over again. She remained adamant that there was nothing I could do and left telling me that she would tell her peers at her doctoral program what a horrible disappointment the training experience had turned out to be.

A discussion with Lissa's training director to deal with this abrupt resignation from the internship revealed that Lissa had experienced problems of this kind continuously during her graduate program. She presented well at interviews and then performed marginally in clinical settings. Accusations of faculty and supervisors having personal animus and racist bias toward her were common. When I queried the difference between this information, which if I had known it would have resulted in Lissa's not being accepted into our internship program, and the content of letters of recommendation for her from her faculty and the training director, I was informed the training director had been advised by the school's legal counsel that she could not discuss the matter further. Implied was that Lissa had threatened or taken legal action against her program. The training director's parting comment was that the school had hoped that, because of our feminist orientation, Lissa would have finally had a different experience with us than in other, more-authoritarian settings. The school could tell me nothing further, bound as they were by confidentiality. I heard later from trainees from Lissa's program who did come to our clinic that she had indeed bad-mouthed our setting, her other supervisors, and me specifically, which as one new trainee said, "Didn't add to her credibility with me, since Shin-Shin (an Asian American former trainee from the same doctoral program) loved this place, and she's usually more accurate about people than Lissa is." This was a painful and somewhat chronically unresolved ending to a difficult process. Empowering Lissa was beyond my skills.

Trainee Impairment or Skill Deficit

Trainees who might otherwise be functional emotionally can at times become impaired because of abuse of substances, illness, prescribed medications' side effects, or difficulties with self-care in the context of severely stressful life circumstances. In addition, the material of psychotherapy can evoke distressing affects or serve as cues for memories of the trainee therapist's own traumatic experiences. Research on practicing psychologists has indicated that significant numbers of professionals are themselves survivors of childhood trauma (Pope & Feldman-Summers, 1992), and a history of depression is also more common among psychologists, according to some research, than in the general population.

A feminist model of supervision starts with the assumptions that psychological distress is normal in response to difficult life events; recreational use of a substance during an intern's nonwork hours is a choice that she or he, as an adult, is free to make so long as she or he is not drunk, high, or hung over when work starts; and illness happens, and a feminist training site has a norm that people take off enough time to get well. The paradigm of the "wounded healer" (Brown, 2012a; Bryan, 2012) is one that is central to feminist therapy supervision because it defines all parties in the process as continuously healing from whatever wounds, historical or current, that allow them to deepen in empathy with psychologically wounded individuals.

Nonetheless, there are circumstances in which this norm of respect for people's choices and privacy becomes a training issue. Such instances occur when the supervisee's capacity to function in a client's best interests is repeatedly affected as distress crosses into impairment of capacities to safely practice. The challenge for feminist supervision is to monitor this bright line in a context in which the norm is a nonauthoritarian one and yet the power of the supervisor to declare certain behaviors unacceptable for practice is maintained.

The model that the feminist supervisor needs to use in the instance of trainee impairment is that of empowering the person to have the best training experience and professional outcomes possible. In this framework, it is best not to have a disciplinary experience and better to have a learning experience. It is best not to harm clients and better to learn how to repair ruptures with clients. It is best not to risk being dismissed from the training site and better to learn how to integrate difficult feedback. If a trainee is impaired she or he may lack the judgment to understand how she or he is undermining the potential for optimal training outcomes or how she or he is disempowering herself or himself through subpar practice and consistently less-than-effective responses to supervisory feedback. When and if a trainee exhibits this degree of impairment, a feminist supervisor must find strategies that require a more directive or consequences-based supervisory intervention for empowerment of a trainee at those times when the trainee's judgment is too impaired to be sufficiently self-protective with regard to undesirable consequences of her or his actions.

A feminist model of supervision provides a clear, a priori message to trainees that distress is normal and expected, self-care is integrated and supported, and impairment differs from distress and will be responded to differently. Any supervision context should have clear information for those being supervised regarding what crossing the line from distress to impairment entails and differentiates intervening with impairment from disciplinary action. This last is important if the intervention is to remain as empowering as possible for the trainee and as collaborative as possible while protecting the welfare of clients.

Feminist supervisory models also include the use of supervisor self-disclosure about personal experiences of distress and of becoming at risk of being impaired. Self-disclosure in the interest of the person being served is a core construct in feminist therapy ethics (Feminist Therapy

Institute, 1990, 1999). This intervention of self-disclosure of personal risk in the supervision context is a strategy for empowerment of supervisees via modeling of transparency and openness regarding a supervisor's own experiences of normative struggle. Too frequently, psychologists in training positions, in the service of maintaining tight boundaries with those they supervise, fail to consider ways in which supervisor self-disclosure might reduce shame and empower trainees to be open about distress before it turns into impairment (Brown & Walker, 1990). An example of how feminist supervision can be a form of impairment prevention is presented here.

I experienced a 2-year period of severe depression in the late 1990s in the context of a painful and shameful combination of professional and personal difficulties and losses (Brown, 2012a). In addition to now writing and speaking publicly about my experience with other therapists as a strategy for reducing our collective silence about our own experiences of distress, I routinely share things about this episode with trainees early in our relationship to illustrate several points. First, I talk about how I had gotten into my difficult place through some persistent failures of self-care. I use the metaphor of me hoping that my trainees will not have to reinvent the wheels of learning self-care that were, for me, forged in the fires of those terrible years of my life. Second, I am transparent about the fact that I, a respected and powerful person in the lives of my supervisees, had a period in my recent life in which my ability to practice was affected by my personal distress. I make visible the effects of my depressed mood and psychosocial challenges on my capacity to show up for my work so that they can more compassionately observe these markers in themselves should they arise. I am, as a colleague has said, "translucent" about myself: not so transparent as to violate my own privacy boundaries but sufficiently visible so as to convey the realities of my struggles without avoiding hard facts. Third, I talk about the various strategies I employed to reduce risks to my clients (getting consultation, getting personal psychotherapy and medication, transferring care of clients whose emotional needs I could not adequately respond to, taking extended time off from my practice on short-term disability leave), and those I generated as longer-term, self-care strategies (taking up martial arts, learning a mindfulness practice, changing my client load so that I could manage the vicarious traumatization without becoming impaired). I tell my trainees: "been there, done that, have the ugly t-shirt, so that you don't have to have that experience; learn from my errors."

This disclosure functions to deshame distress, as discussed earlier in this book, and to normalize and raise consciousness about our collective risk for distress as psychotherapists that can rise to impairment and boundary crossing or violation (Peterson, 1992). It also has the effect of creating less of a power differential for supervisees when their issues of distress and risk of impairment arise because it removes the illusion that the supervisor has no experience of such struggle.

Still, there will be instances in which the supervised person's slide from distress to impairment has been unpreventable, no matter how much care and self-care are available. Those are times when a supervisor must find ways to empower through nurturance and protectiveness, both of which imbalance the power dynamic for a short period. An example of this follows.

Drew, a cisgender male Euro American therapist from a lower middle class family working in private practice saw me for ongoing consultation on the treatment of complex trauma survivors. He had always practiced in safe manner and was apparently in adequate mental and physical health. He had signed my consultation contract (see Appendix C), which allowed me to intervene in his practice should I have concerns about impairment. Both my consultee and I practice in a state where professionals are now required by law to report suspected impairment by a health professional to their licensing authority unless the professional in question is one's psychotherapy client, and the contract gave informed consent to him regarding this mandatory reporting rule.

About a decade into our consultation work, during which we worked together well and productively, processed many dynamics related to our differences across intersectionalities, and got to know one another slightly as people beyond our professional roles, he began to show up late for appointments, which was unlike him, and to seem confused and disorganized during our meetings. When I asked him what was going on, he was atypically avoidant and vague, referring to some medical problems for which he was being worked up diagnostically. I expressed my concern about what I was observing and asked him to keep me apprised of what the testing showed, wishing him well, and sharing my hope that nothing serious would come out of the tests.

At our next meeting, a month later, he seemed to smell of alcohol. At this point, I expressed my concern that he was engaging in some form of self-destructive behavior, sharing that he would be disempowering himself quite utterly were he to be acting in his sessions with clients in the manner he was acting with me. I was scared for him that day, and I let him see that.

I asked him what was happening, and he told me that it was personal and none of my business. He let me know in clear terms that he thought I was crossing a line that felt inappropriate to him by commenting on his mental state, despite my having done so many times in the past. I let him know that I was worrying, given the constellation of behaviors that had culminated in his coming to our meeting smelling of alcohol, that he might be impaired and that I wanted us to together call the state hotline for impaired health professionals so that he could self-report and be evaluated by them. We both knew that such self-report would protect him from disciplinary action against his license, and I reaffirmed that fact to him. I told him that I was frightened that he was about to create serious difficulties for himself professionally that might lead to formal discipline and that I knew he could avoid those by becoming involved with the impaired professional program. I was transparent about my care for him and my worry about what I was seeing and hearing.

His response was to storm out of the office, which itself was evidence to me that he probably had become impaired because he had never previously been even the least resistant to difficult feedback from me. I called him later that day and left a message on his voicemail to the effect that I would be glad to contact the hotline together with him but that if I did not hear back by the end of the week about making a date to do so, I would follow the legal mandate for me to report my concern that he might be impaired. I told him that I preferred not to go that route, which seemed authoritarian and noncollaborative to me, and again expressed my heart-felt worries that he was about to put his career at risk and his license on the line. I kept trying to empower him.

When he did not call me back by the end of the week, I made the call to the hotline. I kept my observations to what I had observed and shared that this practitioner's problem behaviors seemed new ones and inconsistent with his previous behaviors. He left one angry message on my voicemail castigating me for having made the report. Two months later, he requested an appointment with me to "make amends and appreciate what you did."

When we met, he told me that, after my call, he had been contacted and assessed by a team from the impaired professionals program and mandated into treatment for the substance abuse that had emerged later in life in the context of a collection of painful personal life stresses and losses, all of which I knew about and all of which he had managed to cope with until the prior 6 months, when his substance use worsened. He apologized for having been secretive with me and talked about how much shame he had experienced as his life and use of marijuana and alcohol spun out of control. I told him how appreciative I was of his having come to me with this amends, noting that despite the norms of 12-step recovery, of which he was now a part, he could have chosen to put off this meeting. I reminded him that I was no stranger to emotional difficulties affecting my practice and expressed my sorrow that something between us had pre-vented him from asking me for more help.

Drew and I talked about how to further heal this rupture. I expressed my curiosity about how I might have been able to make it more possible for him to share his struggles with me, exploring obstacles that might have been inherent in my style as a consultant to his being more empowered to speak truth and seek help. Drew shared his perspective that his own nar-ratives of masculinity and shame over supposed weakness in the presence of a woman had been central to his inability to seek help from me earlier in his struggles. I acknowledged that I had failed to actively consider and raise those matters, even though they had been a central focus of discus-sion between us early in our relationship. We agreed that we would pro-ceed in our consultation relationship and continue to repair the rupture by exploring in an ongoing manner the ways in which our joint inattention to gender dynamics in our relationship had become a barrier to Drew's being able to get the support he needed. We also agreed that we would begin our meetings with a check-in as to his recovery process, specifically as it affected his work as a psychotherapist. Drew has remained clean and sober for several years now and became a peer mentor in a program for other substance-affected health and mental health professionals, sharing his "experience, strength, and hope" about the value of asking for help. We both agree that had I not taken the step to actively intervene, he would have made the kind of clinical errors that are potentially career-ending.

POWER AND EVALUATION
IN FEMINIST SUPERVISION

As noted throughout this book, the analysis of power dynamics in relationships, including that between supervisor and supervisee, is an explicit, foregrounded component of feminist practice. The role power of the supervisor in relationship to the supervisee, of both therapists to the client, and of the client to the therapist-in-training should have been a topic of discussion early and often in supervision. Long before issues of evaluation of the supervisee's work become salient, the supervision will have addressed ways in which the client experiences and expresses power and powerlessness, and parallel processes and experiences for the trainee. In addition, the supervisor will have modeled understanding power and disempowerment through transparency of personal experience. Collaboration and empowerment will have been consistent themes for the supervisory experience.

Because the trainee will have had good quality informed consent to the evaluative aspects of the supervisory relationship, she or he will have clear expectations of how feedback will be given and how problematic behaviors on the part of a trainee will be addressed by this supervisor or training site. The feminist supervisor models the both/and dialectic of empowering the trainee while needing to retain evaluative authority for the protection of all parties in the supervisory triad.

Positive evaluation of trainee performance should be occurring at every single supervisory encounter to counter the insidious effects of disempowerment and disrespect with which a trainee routinely deals. Such positive evaluation needs to be specific and focused, and related to what the trainee has identified as helpful feedback. The supervisor must be aware that positive feedback and evaluation is a stance of greater power and thus actively solicit feedback from the trainee about whether supervision is being helpful. A feminist supervisor remains aware of ways in which aspects of identity and personal experience may make it difficult for a trainee to receive and internalize positive feedback on her or his work and also makes the time and space available for a trainee to process this kind of difficult feedback. The trainee who struggles with a narrative of never being adequate or not living up to hypothetical potential may not be able, at first, to see her or himself mirrored positively by the supervisor.

In addition, the feminist supervisor may value characteristics in a trainee that have been punished or shamed in other educational settings, particularly when those characteristics are ones associated with target group membership. For instance, a trainee who has been shamed by non-feminist faculty or supervisors for being "too empathic" with clients or chastised for being "too political" in her or his analysis of a client's concerns is likely to be, like Charlie Brown with the football, wondering when Lucy-the-supervisor is going to pull acceptance out from under, and thus initially may be reluctant to accept the positive evaluation.

This same dialectic applies when a feminist supervisor needs to give critical feedback to a trainee. The feedback is designed to be both critical *and* empowering. The focus of giving remedial feedback should be on using this as an opportunity to increase trainee empowerment via the enhancement of competence and clinical capacities. The feminist supervisor questions herself or himself as to how to give difficult feedback in a manner that is calculated to reduce shame and normalize the nature of the problem, tie the feedback to the trainee's own stated goals and values for professional development, and have as a goal of critical feedback that the trainee does not simply remediate the problem but reaches a more advanced and sophisticated level of practice as a result of the remediation and critical feedback.

The feminist supervisor can also model the experience of learning through error during the process of giving critical feedback to a supervisee by teaching from her or his own mistakes. Although this should be a component of good supervision no matter what the supervisor's theoretical orientation, the explicit theory underlying the use of teaching from one's own clinical errors is that of consciousness raising regarding the realities of psychotherapy practice and creating the image of the shared world of psychotherapists to which the supervisor is inviting the supervisee with this combination of critical feedback and self-disclosure.

Thus, a feminist supervisor will be explicit about critical feedback being a process that aggravates the power differential and will explore, in collaboration with the trainee and if possible other feminist supervisors, how to minimize the distortion of power differentials so that critical and remedial feedback is not an experience of disempowerment. Feedback should be behaviorally specific and descriptive, and remedial steps should be similarly framed, with clear timelines that take into account the realities of the trainee's capacities and social context as well as those of the training setting.

The following is an excerpt, edited to deidentify the intern (including the use of no pronouns that could point to gender), of a remediation document created at my feminist therapy training clinic for an intern who planned to work as a therapist in the small community of which the intern was an active member. I was concerned about the trainee's ability to understand and safely practice in the context of role overlap in small communities. Early in the placement, the trainee had made several naïve clinical errors in relationship to the issue of multiple and overlapping social roles about which the trainee had difficulty hearing corrective feedback, in part because of the trainee's passion for serving the community of which the intern was a part. I could empathize deeply; I had a similar commitment to serving lesbian communities as a goal for my own training and had made enough mistakes in my early years of practice to have some good ideas about how to manage overlap well, but I also knew how one could make errors that would blow back onto the therapist in painful ways. I genuinely wanted to protect this trainee from some of that sort of misery, and I wanted to support the trainee's goal of serving a stigmatized and underserved population.

However, several months into internship, the trainee continued to exhibit the same level of naïveté and make similar errors of judgment, and appeared to be resistant to and not learning from feedback. In consultation with the other in-house supervisor, I prepared a feedback document stating the following:

> Interns are expected to demonstrate understanding of the ethics and boundaries of psychotherapy. You are preparing to practice in a context (e.g., small community with many role overlaps) where attention to boundaries becomes particularly important to safe practice for you and your clients. Your demonstrated understanding of the importance of boundaries in therapy as a therapeutic issue, rather than as simply a set of constraining rules, as demonstrated by (here I describe the supervisory encounters that had raised my concern) is not consistent with what I know to be your sophisticated abilities to think about power and ethics in therapy. My observation is that you are treating these norms as a problem rather than as the safe container for therapy that they are. Because of your career goals, and because of my own extensive knowledge of working in such small communities, I am often worried by what I hear you voice about these matters and frightened for you when I notice you not wanting or able to take in feedback from me about this topic.

Note the tone of this document; it is one of concern and shared values, with an emphasis on wanting the trainee to remain safe and effective. It notes the trainee's strengths and links the development of this skill to those strengths, rather than simply singling out the area requiring remediation and not acknowledging the trainee's capacities.

The trainee was assigned to read several articles on role overlap in small communities and to write an essay conveying what had been learned about how to effectively and safely practice in settings where there is extensive social role overlap between clients and therapists. I hoped that by making me less the source of the message, and giving the trainee the chance to read (a preferred learning strategy) and digest in privacy, outside of the potentially activating interpersonal context of our relationship, it would become more possible for the trainee to acquire and internalize the necessary information.

Again, notice that the focus of this remedial process was concern for the *supervisee's* welfare in current and future practice. My attempts to empower the trainee to practice safely included my searching for alternate strategies for teaching about this topic, taking myself out of the role of expert, and placing the authors of the articles in that position. When we discussed this matter, the supervisee raised the concern that I was not allowing the supervisee to make mistakes and was infantilizing in my feedback. I acknowledged and validated that I was not allowing this person to make the kinds of mistakes that I had made. I shared that I was extremely protective of the supervisee and in fact all of the people I train and that because I had several painful experiences with naïvely mishandled role overlap early in my career, I was perhaps more motivated than would be many supervisors to shield this supervisee from similar experiences and to offer mentorship on this issue that I had not received from supervisors. I apologized if my protectiveness came across as infantilizing and told the supervisee that I recognized my younger self in what the supervisee was saying and doing, both in terms of passion for work and naïveté about how to make the role overlap work for all parties. I again employed self-disclosure as a strategy for dealing with dynamics of power imbalance. This exchange appeared to have transformed the remedial process into one in which the supervisee could feel my care in the form of my close identification with the supervisee's experiences, rather than solely feeling judged and distanced from by me.

I decided to take a risk so as to level the power even more and went into some detail about one of my most foolish and risky adventures in mismanagement of role overlap in small communities during my first 2 years of practice. I hoped that my willingness to model transparency and teach from my own errors added a level of power balance to the critical feedback process and increased the sense of identification and solidarity. The supervisee appeared, as a result of reading the articles, more able to see my motivation for making this issue a topic of formal concern and went on to write a thoughtful essay on role overlap that demonstrated a deepening of knowledge, as well as a more mature and sophisticated appraisal of the issue than had been previously exhibited in supervision.

MULTICULTURAL AND DIVERSITY ISSUES

Feminist therapy is an inherently and, since the early 2000s, explicitly multicultural theory of psychotherapy (Brown, 2010). Feminist therapists practice from an understanding that all people have multiple and intersecting identities. Feminist therapy has been influenced by the work of feminist multicultural identity theorists such as Hays (2008) and Root (1998, 2000), and by feminist/womanist theorists of the identities of women of color (Comas-Díaz & Greene, 2013) and feminist students of narratives of masculinity (Englar-Carlson & Stevens, 2006). The last two decades of feminist therapy theory and practice have been marked by an increasing attention to issues beyond gender, including ethnicity, culture, social class, sexual orientation, disability and ability, and the meanings of indigenous status, histories of colonization, and experiences of emigration and dislocation. All of the epistemologies of feminist therapy have as a goal the therapist's capacity to generate a more highly attuned response to the needs of diverse individuals.

Following on these feminist models of intersectionality of identities (Enns, Williams, & Fassinger, 2013), feminist supervisors explore with trainees the diverse meaning and implications of their own identities. The feminist epistemology of diversity is not of the privileged person working with the *other*, which is the manner in which issues of multiculturalism and diversity are most commonly taught in graduate education, but instead a paradigm of one individual with a particular combination of identities, power, privilege, internalized oppression and disadvantage, working with another person with a different and sometimes similar collection of identities, supervised by a third individual who brings her or his own intersectionalities to the mix.

The feminist supervisor will draw the trainee's attention to ways in which there are varying power dynamics and shifts in the supervision triad. For instance, if the supervisee and the client are both Euro American men and the supervisor is a woman of color, the feminist supervisor's task is to engage the trainee in supervision to consider the ways in which dynamics of gender and ethnicity might create openings as well as challenges for the trainee. The feminist supervisor notes that the trainee is being required by the demand characteristics of supervision to authorize the voice of a person who, in the larger social scheme, is devalued and whose voice, in that other context, is seen as having no authority. He is thus being required to demonstrate humility with regard to race and gender, own his privilege, and notice its effects on his relationship with the supervisor. He is also being asked to integrate that racial and gender humility into his work with someone who may not himself be open to authorizing the power of a woman of color, whether or not she has a doctoral degree. The supervisor, in turn, must observe how she may be responding to subtle nonconscious pulls to either devalue or overvalue what comes from the trainee and his client. All of this the supervisor makes transparent and integrates into observations of the therapy process itself. The therapist and supervisor can wonder together about the unconscious presence of the supervisor in the therapy room and explore together how it may be affecting the client.

A feminist supervisor is alert to the variety of combinations and permutations of difference that can emerge. Remember Carly, the working-class intern? One of our more interesting and evocative exchanges occurred in her work with a woman who was also a member of the working poor. Carly challenged me on my classism regarding suggestions I had for her about self-care strategies to offer to her client. Drawing on her own experiences, she reminded me that the entire notion of self-care seemed to ignore the realities of her life and thus also seemed to her to be ignoring those of her client. We had to engage together around my taking responsibility for my classism and explore what wisdom she brought from experience to the construct of self-care, which as she noted wryly in our next exchange, "should not be reserved only for you folks who grew up in the Mercer Islands of the world" (using the Seattle suburb as a stand-in for upper-middle-class life). The culturally competent feminist supervisor must remain humble and open to challenge from trainees whose intersectionalities may better prepare them for work with a particular client than have the supervisor's.

A feminist supervisor will explore dynamics of alliance between participants in the supervision triad across lines of power and privilege (Mio & Roades, 2003). A goal for a feminist practitioner is to be able to occupy a position of alliance in relationship to clients and colleagues who are in less-advantaged positions in formal social hierarchies and do to so in manners that do not shame or disempower themselves. As discussed earlier, social action as a means of embodying ally identity is one of several strategies a feminist supervisor will discuss with those she or he trains, extending and deepening the alliance model by encouraging trainees to expand their visions of how to express alliance in both direct (in-session) and indirect (in the larger society's) manners.

Finally, the feminist supervisor will introduce issues of the larger social ecology into supervisory conversations about difference and power. The trainee, supervisor, and client all also exist in that external social and political sphere in which the supervisor is continually exposed to microaggressions and insidious trauma and in which both therapist and client may be perpetrators of those wounds. A trainee may also, as an ally, experience the microaggressions against the supervisor. News stories of the murders of unarmed African American men and women by law enforcement are one common source of such microaggression in the lives of supervisors, trainees, and clients of color. A feminist supervisor must be prepared to foreground the effects of this sort of extratherapeutic event on the supervisor–supervisee and therapist–client relationships and on how materials emerging from the therapy are handled. Thus, the feminist supervisor must develop heightened levels of cultural competence around issues of transference and countertransference (Brown, 2012b). She or he models effective engagement in difficult dialogues around issues of difference in the context of supervision so that the trainee internalizes the possibilities of managing such dialogues in the treatment room.

LEGAL AND ETHICAL ISSUES: FEMINIST THERAPY ETHICS IN ACTION

A feminist supervisor will expose trainees to the Feminist Therapy Institute's Code of Ethics (Appendix D) and engage trainees in discussions about topics that are particularly germane to feminist practice in addition to ensuring compliance with the codes of the supervisor's and trainee's relevant professional organizations. These topics in feminist therapy ethics include what constitutes a frame for feminist practice: the use of self-disclosure as an empowerment strategy, dealing with role overlap in small communities, and therapist self-care (Brown, 1991; Lerman & Porter, 1990). A feminist supervisor also will introduce trainees to notions of social justice ethics, which are differentiated from the legalistic ethics of the American Psychological Association (APA), and to critical thinking regarding the assumptions underlying the ethics codes of the mental health professions (Brown, 1995, 1997). Feminist supervisors will invite critical thinking about ethics by introducing other ethical models such as, for example, that of the Canadian Psychological Association, which uses a more-relational, less-legalistic framework than does the APA, and which mandates self-care for psychotherapists. A feminist supervisor will not simply guide trainees to follow ethics codes and look for minimal compliance with the letter of the law. Rather, she or he will engage with trainees to explore how ethics codes of their professions empower or disempower and how they uphold or challenge oppressive norms in dominant cultures. Feminist supervisors can, in particular, use case examples from current and ongoing controversies in the field to illustrate the dynamic tensions between the feminist ethic of empowerment and mainstream psychological ethics of risk management via compliance with carefully worded rules.

Dealing With Role Overlap

Communities of therapists are, like other small communities, ones in which roles may overlap among social, personal, and professional worlds. This is particularly true when all parties in the supervisory mix identify as feminists and participate in some way in feminist community and social activities in which they encounter one another in different roles than those in the supervisory relationship. Fortunately, feminist therapy theory has been discussing the ethics of managing role overlap for three decades (Berman, 1985; Brown, 1985, 1994, 2010), which means that feminist supervisors have specific guidance in developing decision strategies for dealing with role overlap.

The specific question addressed is one of how or whether sharing social and personal spaces empowers or disempowers the more vulnerable parties in the exchange. Supervisors who anticipate role overlap should initiate conversations with trainees regarding potential realms of overlap and engage collaboratively with the trainee to develop strategies that support both parties' well-being. The supervisor has the responsibility in these matters to prioritize the welfare of the more vulnerable party and explore what options are available for meeting her or his own needs when it appears that role overlap might put the welfare of the trainee in jeopardy. The supervisor also needs to assess whether participation in some areas of role overlap is in her or his own best interest.

As an example, interns on the staff at a feminist training clinic were offered an opportunity to participate in an experiential therapy training program in which participants engaged in heightened levels of emotionally risky behaviors as part of acquiring the intervention model. One of the clinic's junior supervisors asked to participate in the training group and discovered that the presence of a supervisor, even someone who self-perceived as a near-peer to the interns, muted the capacity of the trainees to fully participate in the training process. The supervisor also found it difficult to utilize the new model because willingness to take emotional risks in the presence of people the supervisor was evaluating was undermined as much for the supervisor as for the interns in the group. In post-hoc analysis of what had not gone well, all parties realized they had not sufficiently explored the risks for all of them of having the supervisor in the training group.

Conversely, in a situation in which an intern and a supervisor were both participants in a group for white women working on overcoming their own racism, the shared vulnerability and experience of transparency in the group had a salutary effect. In this instance, the two parties had carefully explored, before the inception of the group, the risks and benefits of both parties participating and developed safeguards for each woman that would protect the supervisory relationship when, as expected from their pregroup discussions, conflict emerged in the group that highlighted differences between the supervisor and the trainee.

In the nonprofessional realm, feminist supervisors collaborate with trainees to develop a shared understanding of boundary management in social and personal overlap settings. Supervisors and trainees who are members of the same religious or political group or who are in the same small communities of faith, ethnicity, or sexual orientation are faced with dilemmas similar to and different from those encountered by feminist therapists dealing with clients and role overlap. If a supervisor sees a trainee affected by substances or behaving poorly in a shared social setting, the supervisor must be cautious about how she or he brings that knowledge into the supervisory relationship. At the least, the supervisor empowers the trainee by being transparent about what she or he has observed, about her or his emotional responses to it, and any ruptures generated by what has been learned in the external situation that might require repair. To avoid stigmatizing the trainee for behaviors that occur away from work, the feminist supervisor should also seek consultation to manage whatever difficult affects are evoked.

Therapist Self-Care

Self-care is a mandatory, not optional, component of psychotherapy practice. Yet in the United States, the only organization that has ever mentioned self-care as an ethical imperative has been the Feminist Therapy Institute. The Canadian Psychological Association's Ethics Code has, as noted, several sections on self-care, but neither the APA nor any other major mental health organization in the United States mentions the topic.

Self-care is a complex phenomenon that extends well beyond the superficial to matters of existential import. The life of a trainee psychologist is often constructed so as to be inimical to self-care: classes that last until well in the evening, practicum and internship sites that use trainees as unpaid labor with the most difficult and demanding clients, and absence of consequences for faculty members or supervisors who use humiliation as a pedagogical strategy are all so common as to be almost assumed as norms by many trainees. Many early career practicing psychologists, particularly those graduating from professional schools, enter the profession with crippling burdens of educational debt in the context of fierce competition for business and systemic barriers to participation in systems of third-party payment. New faculty members on the tenure track are expected to sacrifice all for their publication record, given that continued employment depends on cranking out publications even if one's relationships or health are put at risk.

All of this is to say that there are many structural and systemic obstacles to self-care in the lives of trainees and those early in their careers, the people who are most likely to cross the path of the feminist supervisor. Add to these other aspects of identity that may make self-care challenging, and it's little wonder this feminist ethical issue can be a thorny one. A feminist supervisor attempts to integrate self-care for the trainee into the supervision process, attending to openings in the life of the trainee or the supervisor that illustrate how essential it is, and supporting the supervisee's appropriate use of self-care strategies. Thus, a supervisor may direct a stressed trainee to take time off and ensure that this occurs without risk or penalty. Feminist supervisors should model self-care and discuss frankly with trainees ways in which they struggle with this. My trainee staff and I have gently and humorously remind one another that no one wants to have her or his eulogy include she or he "never took a day off."

Social Justice Ethics

As noted earlier, feminist supervisors inculcate trainees in the construct of social justice ethics. This overarching ethical strategy in which feminist ethics are embedded intersects with and supersedes professional ethics codes by situating the practices of psychotherapy and psychological assessment within the larger questions of what oppresses and what liberates people. There are aspects of all professional ethics codes that are largely present for the protection of the members of the profession (Brown, 1997; Payton, 1994). Feminist supervision invites trainees to think critically about those aspects of their ethics codes, consider the question of who is truly benefited, and to what degree benevolence becomes a cloak for parentalism or protection of the guild and thus turns into claims supporting hierarchies of power and dominance in relationships between professionals and their clients or students. The ethics of social action, as discussed elsewhere in this book, are also part of what feminist supervision brings under the rubric of ethics education in supervision: questions of how to most effectively marshal protest actions against unjust societal conditions; how to be an ally with people who are members of target groups, particularly groups consisting of psychotherapy consumers; and how to integrate social justice activism into one's daily psychotherapy practice are all components of the social justice ethic that emerges during feminist supervision.

As an example, I have discussed with trainees the social justice implications of becoming an impaneled provider for insurance companies and government programs such as Medicare or the Affordable Care Act. We consider issues of social justice for clients in terms of access for those who have coverage but not funds, and of social justice for providers who experience the value of their work diminished by the metrics used by third-party payers to calculate the value of a psychotherapist's work. We consider the values and costs of offering pro bono or low-cost services, and analyze the challenges to doing so in manners that do not shame their recipients for being poor or undermine the therapist's capacity to feel sufficiently safe economically. In the realm of psychological assessment, we discuss how to frame interpretations of formal assessment so that the findings will be presented honestly and in manners that do not disempower clients or place them at unnecessary risk in legal or educational systems. We talk about the *golden rule* paradigm for writing case notes: "Write not about your client the sort of things you would not want your therapist writing about you in the notes of your therapy sessions."

Defining these and similar decisions in terms of an ethics of social justice and encouraging trainees to see how each of their professional decisions can and does have social justice meaning are components of how feminist ethics are integrated into the feminist supervision setting. Expanding the notion of justice beyond its legalistic meanings and into the relational realm and exploring how decisions become more just when they are more empowering are specific components of feminist supervision on ethical matters.

Trainees can also be provided with formal training in becoming social justice agents. Goodman, Liang, Helms, Latta, Sparks, and Weintraub (2004) describe a programmatic effort, the "first year experience," in the Boston College Counseling Psychology doctoral program to train students in feminist and multicultural methods of social justice action. They discuss the challenges and rewards of the effort and some of the dilemmas that emerged as faculty and students worked at integrating psychological and social action roles.

The program was not done in the context of psychotherapy supervision but rather with students working in the community in roles involving prevention work, interprofessional collaboration, and advocacy, and being supervised both on-site in the community and by Boston College faculty. The authors comment on the degree to which these experiences were consciousness raising for the students, demonstrating how to put social justice ethics into effect. The program offers a paradigm for feminist supervision that broadens the definition of what is supervised while retaining the emphasis on empowering the trainee and those receiving services from her or him.

Handling Conflicts in Supervision

Although there is no specifically feminist methodology for approaching conflicts between supervisors and those we supervise, there are specifically feminist questions that, if asked, may assist in the resolution of conflict. As discussed earlier with regard to problematic trainees, there are a variety of pathways by which supervisor and supervisee can arrive at a conflict, including systemic factors encouraging differences, actual differences between the parties involved regarding what is best for a client, and supervisor and supervisee personal dynamics that can lead to conflictual interactions.

The specifically feminist questions have to do with these variables. Is the conflict occurring because the demand characteristics of the situation are leading the supervisor to behave in a more authoritarian manner that is violating supervisee beliefs and creating feelings of betrayal? Are differences in external experiences of power and privilege leading to distrust or breakdowns in communication? Supervision across difference can evoke anxiety in all parties, which may heighten initially as a result of the supervisor naming the issues of difference (Nelson, Gizara, Hope, Phelps, Steward, & Weitzman, 2006). Inherent in these questions is the assumption that both parties are contributing to and thus both are responsible for arriving at solutions for the conflict that occurs and that the supervisor, by virtue of greater role power, has heightened responsibilities to be transparent and self-reflexive. As true in all aspects of feminist supervision, the goal is a liberatory one, in which conflict is not resolved through silencing or compliance on the part of either party; instead, both the process and the outcome model feminist understanding of rupture repair in therapy. A feminist supervisor's commitment is to make the conflict with the trainee grist for the mill of the learning experience, exploring how the conflict informs the trainee about what happens in her or his therapeutic work, making transparent ways in which this conflict parallels those that the supervisor has with clients or other trainees, and modeling how the person with greater role power initiates conflict resolution and repair of the rupture.

Some conflicts between a supervisor and trainees do not resolve, as we saw with the example of Lissa. One of the challenges of the feminist supervisory model is that it may activate distress in some trainees; they may experience too little structure, too much autonomy, or come to supervision with the distorted expectation that *feminist* equals *nonjudgmental*. The difficult or impossible-to-resolve supervision conflicts that I and other experienced feminist supervisors have encountered frequently have elements of one or more of these variables. It is not my sense that the feminist model is more inherently likely to evoke these specific conflicts. Rather, I have found it more surprising and challenging for feminist supervisors to work with trainees who seem not to want to be empowered to become their best and most effective professional selves. This parallels one of the continuing challenges of all feminist practice: what to do when someone receiving our services appears, after our careful, thoughtful, and prolonged engagement with them, to not wish to become empowered and effective in their life?

CONCLUSION

Difficulties with supervision are not unique to feminist practice. However, the unique focus in feminist supervision on empowerment offers potential solutions to common difficulties, suggesting that integrating feminist models into other supervisory strategies may assist supervisors of many theoretical orientations in responding to these common difficulties. Whether or not this is the case is a question for research on feminist supervision, which is the topic of the next chapter.

Development of Supervisors, Development of the Field: Future Directions for Feminist Supervision Practice

Being a supervisor is, like any other role taken on by a practicing psychologist, a developmental process. Someone new to supervision has different challenges than a supervisor who has been practicing the art for decades. The novice may be challenged by insufficient confidence or experience with a broad enough range of clients. The experienced supervisor, who has most likely had little formal training and much time in the job, must be attentive to the risk of becoming complacent, not seeing how she or he misses important cues, or mistaking her or his clinical experience for an education in supervision.

For a feminist supervisor, there are additional challenges inherent in the development of one's identity and practice as a feminist and the process by which the supervisor continues to learn about how to integrate feminist political awareness and feminist psychological scholarship into her or his practices. The feminist therapist and supervisor I am in 2015, writing this

http://dx.doi.org/10.1037/14878-006
Supervision Essentials for the Feminist Psychotherapy Model of Supervision, by L. S. Brown

volume, is not the feminist therapist and supervisor who wrote my last two books on feminist therapy and is not the one I will become in the future. To be faithful to her or his commitments as a therapist, a feminist, and a supervisor, the feminist supervisor must find ways to support growth and development in all of these components of her or his supervisory identities.

TRAINING AND DEVELOPMENT OF THE SUPERVISOR

Optimally, a feminist supervisor has had what I did not—formal training during graduate education in models of supervision, including course work and supervision as a supervisor, as well as regular postgraduate continuing education in the skill of supervision. A feminist supervisor in optimal circumstances will additionally have had formal course work in feminist psychology and psychotherapy, as well as supervision from a feminist supervisor. Also optimally, a feminist supervisor seeks and receives regular consultation on her or his supervision practice, including when possible, via direct observation from other feminist supervisors. Feminist supervisors like myself, who had access to none of these optimal conditions, should at a minimum seek consultation from other feminist supervisors in some form.

Cosupervision of a supervision group can provide a strategy for receiving this kind of direct observation while making available modeling of supervision by the cosupervisor. As is true with group supervision, cosupervision of a group creates opportunities for all parties involved to observe sharing of power, handling differences and disagreements, and a wider range of expressions of feminist principles in supervision while simultaneously providing ongoing support to the professional development of the supervisors.

Training for novice supervisors can also take place using this structure. Having a postdoc or advanced doctoral intern or early career professional serve as cosupervisor in a group with less-experienced trainees creates a situation in which all parties are transparent in their learning experiences, and the precept that each person has expertise to offer can be embodied in the structure of the supervision group. This model also breaks down expectations of hierarchy and models the empowerment of trainees to take on more challenging roles as they progress in professional development.

However, the aspirational and optimal components of a feminist supervisor's experience are not always available. Thus at a minimum a feminist therapy supervisor should have familiarity with the most recent scholarship on feminist psychological science and psychotherapy and formal training or mentorship via apprenticeship in the role of supervisor. A feminist supervisor should have a strong identity as a feminist therapist, either alone or in addition to other theoretical allegiances (e.g., "feminist and relational psychoanalysis"; "feminist and dialectical behavior therapy (DBT)"; or "feminist and mindfulness-based therapies" are descriptions of some of the feminist supervisors of my acquaintance).

SUPERVISOR STRESS AND DISTRESS

Supervision is, at its best, a real joy and at its worst, a source of anxiety, self-doubt, and frustration. At its best, it informs the psychotherapy practice of the supervisor, reminding her or him about the core skills of psychotherapy, requiring the supervisor to attend more closely to her or his own work so as to teach from that experience. At its worst, it is a miserable experience of sitting with a difficult trainee who responds poorly to supervision and engenders feelings of helplessness and hopelessness, guilt and shame in the supervisor. I have probably had more sleepless nights because of problems with a trainee than I have ever had because of work as a psychotherapist. When supervision is going badly, more is at stake: the welfare of the trainee, the welfare of the client, and the supervisor's license all can be put in peril.

Supervisors also practice in the context of their own lives. Family members age and require care, people die, relationships go through rough patches or dissolve, children are born. Our own illness and infirmity creep up on us. The increasingly experienced supervisor is also the aging supervisor, at risk for dementia. All supervisors, no matter what our theory of therapy and supervision, have a responsibility to have regular consultation with peers and colleagues who are explicitly empowered to tell us when we look and sound as if we are approaching being in trouble. One of the risks inherent in being a psychotherapist who is sufficiently experienced to be in the position to offer supervision is that the requirement that one receive some kind of regular oversight of one's work melts away, especially if one is practicing outside of an institution. Although the importance of having peer oversight of some kind into one's work is not a specifically feminist construct, it does rest conceptually within the feminist ethic requiring self-care for the practitioner. Exposing oneself to license revocation in the wake of encroaching dementia or debilitating depression is shaming and a failure of self-care. Agreeing to have a colleague who is allowed to "take away the keys" when she or he detects that we are no longer able to "drive" the vehicle of our practice is planning for self-care rather than allowing ourselves to become ineffective.

All of these factors of life can become components of supervisor stress and risk for impairment. Feminist practice conceptualizes this less as burnout and more in terms of *vicarious traumatization* (VT) (Pearlman & Saakvitne, 1995). VT is constructed as a relational dynamic arising from continuing and repeated experiences of genuine empathic connection with individuals in distress. Defining the potentially exhausting experiences inherent in longtime practice as relational rather than as about some defect in the psychotherapist is consistent with feminist constructs of reciprocal influence in the therapeutic relationship. Unlike burnout, VT is defined as both inevitable and mitigatable in process. If understood, VT does not need to become a problem for the practitioner. Thus, the model is that the practitioner cannot *not* be transformed by relationships with clients (and by inference, supervisees) but is empowered to notice this experience of transformation compassionately, see it as normative, and engage in strategies for making those effects helpful rather than hurtful.

For supervisors, VT comes from encounters with clients and those being supervised. Ironically, the supervision relationships may have more effect because of the developing collegial relationship and the potential for the supervisee to enter the supervisor's professional and/or personal circles at some date in the future. The possibility exists for full and genuine emotional connection between trainees and their supervisors, and with that comes the potential for more intense emotional experiences in those relationships. The feminist construct of covision and reciprocal influence suggests that feminist supervisors should not construe their supervisory work as somehow lighter or less likely to have emotional impact than their psychotherapy practice.

The topic of supervisor impairment is difficult to address no matter what the theoretical model of those involved. The people most likely to observe such impairment are supervisees, who are in positions of less power and heightened risk should they attempt to bring their concerns to the attention of the supervisor about whom they are worried. The stories shared with me by colleagues and friends about supervisors who were drunk, sexually harassed one of us, fell asleep during supervision, or seemed forgetful at a level suggesting cognitive impairment are all evidence of the reality that supervisors, like psychotherapists, sometimes practice when impaired.

Theoretically, the feminist model, by empowering trainees, might embolden them to bring concerns to a supervisor's attention. Realistically, this is an unlikely scenario; no matter how much the feminist supervisor empowers trainees, the latter are still in vulnerable positions, needing good evaluations and letters of recommendation from the supervisor. I recall with some pain being contacted by a former client, now in graduate school, about her supervisor, a person known to me, who was descending into late-stage alcoholism and becoming abusive toward my former client when the supervisor was drunk. My former client felt trapped and terrified; the supervisor was a highly visible feminist psychologist who absolutely would have penalized my former client, now the other person's trainee, for bringing it up. We ended up discussing how to be as self-protective as possible while finding ways for my former client to transfer to a different supervisor.

However, by modeling strategies for approaching impaired colleagues and discussing this as a part of professional development with trainees, a feminist supervisor empowers trainees to be able to develop effective strategies for responding should the feminist supervisor become impaired. Discussing how to overcome one's fear of being a whistleblower, exploring the use of impaired practitioner programs run by professional associations as a means of involving the supervisor's peers while protecting supervisees and students, and making transparent fears regarding retaliation should all be components of how feminist supervisors empower trainees in the maturation of their professional identities.

Supervisors are also capable of developing persistent and problematic reactions to trainees that resemble countertransference. The explicitly feminist aspect of exploring this phenomenon is, like other feminist analysis of countertransference, founded in understanding how the multiple and intersecting identities of supervisor and trainee may be evoking pernicious and problematic emotional responses or overly positive and idealizing ones in the supervisor. Consultation with a colleague about this kind of problematic emotional response to a trainee, if it persists, is also a necessity for the welfare of all parties. Feminist practice also compassionately empowers a supervisor to own simply not liking a particular trainee and to lean on the work of Pope and Tabachnick (1993) regarding aversive affects about clients to inform having similarly aversive feelings about a supervisee.

THE NECESSITY OF ONGOING LEARNING AND CONSULTATION FOR THE SUPERVISOR

Functioning as a supervisor is a mandate to keep on one's toes and remain open to new information; this is true for supervising more than almost any other activity in which a professional psychologist engages. If we are to do the best possible job of creating the next generation of our colleagues, all supervisors have a responsibility to those coming after us to be well-informed by the latest science regarding all aspects of the practice in which we train people.

Nowhere is this truer than in the field of feminist practice, which is still a relatively young discipline in which new information and innovations emerge regularly. Most important in terms of philosophical changes, the entire focus of the field has shifted in the past decade from being solely about women therapists working with women to a more holistic approach that includes clients and therapists from all genders. If a feminist supervisor has not been keeping track of this shift, she or he will fail to adequately inform trainees who are not women that they, too, are of course feminist therapists. Research on psychotherapy with marginalized populations done from a feminist perspective also has grown exponentially, as has our knowledge about ways in which intersectionalities of identities operate. In addition, feminist therapy has been more intentionally integrated with other psychotherapeutic models, such as modern psychoanalytic and object relations approaches, mindfulness-based psychotherapies, and cognitive therapies; no feminist supervisor should, at this time in the early 21st century, be in the position of inventing the wheel of such integration entirely. The infusion of the norm of cultural competence into feminist practice is also relatively more recent. All of this growth and movement in the short time that feminist therapy has been around should serve as the necessary incentive for feminist supervisors to know that their knowledge is not static or finished, so they should actively pursue professional enrichment.

A feminist supervisor should subscribe to and read the two main journals in the field of feminist psychology: *Women and Therapy* and *Psychology of Women Quarterly*. The former is an interdisciplinary journal that is more specifically focused on psychotherapy practice and has historically been the setting in which new ideas in feminist therapy first see the light of day. The journal has excellent special issues on the widest possible range of topics, including the first work on feminist therapy with posttraumatic stress disorder, feminist practice with refugee and immigrant women, and an entire special issue (volume 33, numbers 1–2) on feminist and multicultural supervision that is must reading for all feminist supervisors. *Psychology of Women Quarterly* is a more academic, feminist psychological science journal, the official publication of the Society for the Psychology of Women. For supervisors who work in or with trainees from clinical scientist programs, access to the research in *Psychology of Women Quarterly* may be especially valuable in offering empirical findings about issues such as feminist identity, intersectionalities, and power dynamics framed in ways that will be more useful to clinical scientist trainees.

There are a number of other more specialized journals in the field of feminist practice, such as the *Journal of Feminist Family Therapy*, *Feminism and Psychology*, and *The Feminist Teacher*, that a feminist supervisor may find helpful in supporting her or his intellectual growth and development. In addition, professional journals that do not generally have a focus on feminist practice but offer a great deal of material on psychotherapy supervision, such as *The Counseling Psychologist*, have had special issues on feminist practice and continue to regularly publish articles on related topics.

Several different conferences occur regularly at which in vivo continuing education in feminist practice is available. The Association for Women in Psychology (http://www.awpsych.org) holds an annual conference that is the most concentrated feminist psychology experience available and includes an interdisciplinary and diverse group of presenters and attendees. The Society for the Psychology of Women, a division of the American Psychological Association (APA), offers programming during APA's annual convention, with at least some of that focused specifically on the topic of feminist practice. In addition, feminist practice presentations frequently can be found in the offerings of other APA divisions, such as Counseling Psychology, Psychology of Men and Masculinity, Psychotherapy, and Psychoanalysis, all of which have strong representations of feminist therapists. Sadly, the Feminist Therapy Institute closed several years before the writing of this book, although the many volumes of scholarship engendered by its membership during its more than 30 years of active existence form the bedrock of the literature in feminist therapy.

The Jean Baker Miller Training Institute (http://www.jbmti.org/) at Wellesley College represents a well-established training center for the relational-cultural branch of feminist practice. The Institute offers webinars, on-site workshops for those living in or near the Boston area, and annual week-long intensive seminars with JBMTI faculty and invited experts.

Although the opportunities for formal training in feminist supervision continue to be less than those available for many other supervisory models, psychologists aspiring to be feminist supervisors today now have more options available for direct training in feminist therapy theory and practice. As described in the research reviewed in the next section, it appears that when a supervisor is grounded in feminist therapy theory and able to fluidly practice empowerment strategies and gender and power analysis, she or he has skills that are transferable to the supervisory realm.

RESEARCH SUPPORT AND FUTURE DIRECTIONS

Research in feminist supervision practice is the future direction of feminist supervision. So little formal research has been conducted on this topic that it is not yet possible to offer a strong research base for the integration of feminist psychotherapy principles into supervision per se. Arczynski's (2014) review of this literature is the most contemporaneous with the writing of this volume; she was able to identify five empirical studies in total on the topic of feminist therapy supervision. As a result, this entire book rests on extrapolation into supervisory tasks of feminist psychotherapy models. Unlike many other systems of psychotherapy that have well-developed literatures on supervision, feminist therapy has yielded less than a score of publications on any aspect of feminist supervisory practice, and most of those have been conceptual or theoretical in nature.

What needs to be known about feminist supervision to support its continued development? First, an exploration of the wealth of qualitative information about experiences of feminist supervision from the standpoints of supervisors and trainees alike is needed, a sort of qualitative meta-analysis of themes emerging from the nonempirical work on this topic. The data that emerge from the published qualitative literature do not seem to converge around particular themes. Some of this work looks at women as supervisors, not at feminist supervisors of any gender, conflating sex of supervisor with the possibility that feminist values are brought to bear. In fact, the topic heading of "women supervising women" rather than "feminist supervision" dominates the extant literature (e.g., Mangione, Mears, Vincent, & Hawes, 2011).

Experiences of feminist supervision that occur irrespective of the genders of the parties involved need to be formally explored and interrogated qualitatively with an eye toward generating quantitatively testable hypotheses about what are the essential components of feminist supervision differentiating it from other paradigms. A finding that emerges from the feminist therapy research literature is that explicit integration of feminist frameworks into treatment changes both client satisfaction and outcome. A hypothesis is that feminist supervision, done with the explicit and intentional integration of feminist principles into the process, should have similar results. A good place to begin the exploration of this hypothesis would be through qualitative study of self-identified feminist supervisors. The one empirical study of this question to date (Green & Dekkers, 2010) found that supervisees' reports of their supervisors use of feminist supervisory practices were linked to their own reports of satisfaction with supervision and positive learning outcomes.

Throughout this book, the topic of power, empowerment, and analysis of power dynamics in the supervision relationship has been repeatedly invoked as central to feminist supervision practice. The one qualitative study of 14 supervisors who identified as practicing a feminist multicultural model (Arczynski, 2014) found that the participants identified "dealing with the complexities of power" as a central theme in their supervisory practices. Arczynski further identified subthemes, which she named "having inordinate power in the supervisory role," "complexity of power manifesting in identities and statuses," "having responsibilities within and beyond the supervision relationship," "managing tensions between responsibility, power, and egalitarianism," and "empowering supervisees." These findings are strikingly consistent with what would be predicted by feminist therapy theory and with the material in this book, all written well before my reading of Arczynski's work. She noted, and I agree, that her findings have the potential to articulate a clear and empirically based theoretical framework that could be used to directly train supervisors in applications of feminist or feminist/multicultural supervision strategies. These findings decidedly merit further study with larger samples of self-identified feminist supervisors.

There is also a need for further research to support Szymanski's (2003, 2005) work examining the relationship of a supervisor's feminist values to her or his application of feminist principles in supervision. Szymanski found that in her 135 participants, the closer the supervisor's adherence to feminist values, the more likely the supervisor was to engage in what are hypothesized to be specifically feminist supervision strategies, such as developing collaborative relationships, engaging in power analysis, and integrating issues of diversity and attention to social context into the supervisory process. In addition, Szymanski found that supervisors who identified with feminist therapy were more likely to be female than male; lesbian, gay, or bisexual than heterosexual; and engaged in some form of feminist activism.

Szymanski's findings are provocative in that they support hypotheses regarding how feminist supervisors will behave and also stereotypes about who becomes a feminist supervisor. They raise questions as to how better to engage men, heterosexual people, and people not engaged in feminist activism to adopt feminist supervision models. Her findings also reinforce that a feminist supervisor must have a strong identification with some model of political feminism to demonstrate adherence to paradigms of feminist supervisory practices.

Szymanski and her colleagues have gone far to answer questions about whether the gender of the therapist matters as much as does the supervisor's feminist values and have found that values far outweigh gender, even though male, particularly cisgender male, feminist therapists remain comparatively few in number (Baird, Szymanski, & Ruebelt, 2007; Szymanski, Baird, & Kornman, 2002). They noted the importance for the field of psychotherapy that men be identified as feminist therapists, subverting dominant cultural discourses that assume that feminist values and female gender are isomorphic. They also found that for male trainees, exposure to a feminist supervisor, as well as to feminist colleagues and educators, can be one of the most effective strategies for creating a male feminist therapist.

These questions also dovetail with the arguments made by MacKinnon, Bhatia, Sunderani, Affleck, and Smith (2011), who explored what it means to bring a feminist supervision framework to work with cisgendered male trainees. They considered several dynamics commonly found in narratives of masculinity, including competition, creating space for the safe expression of emotion, and addressing diversity within men's experiences and narratives of masculinities. They suggested that feminist supervision may invite dominant culture male trainees to explore and interrogate those narratives, consider how gender and power dynamics are relevant to understanding themselves and their work, and construct a different image of their own masculinities that can inform their therapeutic work. The article by MacKinnon et al. is entirely theoretical and, like this book, argues for further research, in this case specifically regarding applications of feminist supervision with cisgendered men.

In the subfield of feminist family therapy, Prouty and colleagues (Prouty, 2001; Prouty, Thomas, Johnson, & Long, 2001) studied supervision in feminist family therapy. Their work is interesting because family therapy supervision requires formal training and certification from the American Association for Marriage and Family Therapy (AAMFT) before a person can self-describe to the public as a family therapy supervisor. Thus, AAMFT-approved family therapy supervisors are, unlike most clinical supervisors, individuals who have had specific training in how to supervise.

However, Prouty's work has been qualitative in nature and her participants few in number (N = 8 supervisors in her initial study). Of interest is her description of how feminist family therapy supervisors made decisions to use collaborative versus hierarchical supervision methods in a given supervision session; her findings suggest that the strategy for doing so was itself collaborative so that even when a supervisor behaved in a more hierarchical manner, she or he did so within the collaborative feminist framework.

Prouty described how the feminist supervisors transformed a common family therapy supervisor technique (the call-in, in which the supervisor behind the mirror calls and gives feedback to the therapist during the session) into collaborative interventions. On the surface, the call-in appears inherently hierarchical, but the feminist supervisors conceptualized it as an opportunity to collaborate midprocess. Hierarchical interventions, when employed, were offered in the context of the feminist power analysis provided by the supervisor, so that

> it also appeared that mutual feedback and open and consistent communication from the collaborative supervision contributed to making the hierarchical methods work for (the trainees), as opposed to hierarchical methods used by previous nonfeminist supervisors, which they had experienced as less helpful or even "bad." (2001, p. 92)

These findings underscore the importance of feminist supervision's attention to power and suggest that further research, both qualitative and quantitative, on the effects of using an empowerment strategy for supervision will be valuable not only to the field of feminist practice.

The implications of the little research that has been done on feminist supervision indicates that much remains to be formally and empirically known, and yet much has been intuited and known sufficiently well to emerge in that research. One of the greatest challenges for the entire field of feminist practice is the dearth of postgraduate formal training programs such as those that exist in psychoanalysis, cognitive–behavioral therapy, Gestalt therapy, and family therapy. Consequently, an important future direction for feminist supervision, in the larger context of feminist psychological practice of all kinds, is the development of more formal training programs in feminist practice that will include course work and supervised experiences in feminist supervision.

Finally, a hoped-for future direction for feminist supervision is its integration into other supervisory models. Feminist therapy's theories and practices, once considered radical, have become increasingly integrated into the mainstream of psychotherapy practice. Attention to gender, issues of power, collaboration with clients, and development of more egalitarian relationships are all themes that can be seen surfacing in a number of approaches to treatment that are not explicitly feminist. This is as feminist therapy theorists have hoped: feminist therapy is a model driven by theory, not technique, and is designed to be integrated into the range of psychotherapeutic interventions. Similarly, feminist supervision models appear to offer insights of value to not-explicitly-feminist supervisors. This book serves as an invitation to consider how a feminist model of supervision can inform supervision practice in general.

CONCLUSION

Feminist supervision practice provides opportunities for supervisors and trainees to radically expand the vision of what the supervisory experience can be. By using the core values of empowerment, attention to gender and other aspects of identities, and development of egalitarian relationships, feminist supervisors can foster empowering and effective pathways for the development of culturally competent, self-aware, compassionate psychotherapists. Because feminist practice is inherently integrative (Brown, 2010), these constructs can be woven into a variety of other supervisory models. It is my hope that supervisors will be inspired to ask themselves the feminist question "What is the one small empowering thing that I can do with this trainee" as they apply their own models of supervision.

Appendix A:
Sample Feminist Supervision Evaluation Form

Fremont Community Therapy Project

Intern Evaluation Form

Intern Name: Date:

Supervisor completing this form:

This is the midyear_____ end of year_____ evaluation
(please check one)

Guidelines for Completing This Form

FCTP's assessments of interns are qualitative in nature. Our focus is on
the intern's demonstration of skills and competencies. Supervisors are
encouraged to frame areas needing growth not as deficiencies, but rather
as under-developed competencies requiring further learning and attention. These forms are not where a supervisor should be commenting on

serious problems for the first time; such comments should have already been forwarded to the FCTP Director. The following competencies represent intern's performance on goals of importance to FCTP as an organization; however, you should feel free to add additional commentary that would be helpful to FCTP in assessment of the intern's progress

I. Quality of interpersonal relatedness. Please comment on the intern's capacities to form and sustain relationships with clients. Please give special note to abilities to repair relationships and nourish the therapeutic alliance.

II. Capacity for self-awareness. Please comment on the intern's capacities for insight and self-awareness. Please note the intern's ability to take and integrate challenging feedback from you. Please comment on the intern's demonstrated use of self in relationships with clients.

III. Attention to diversity. Please comment as to intern's demonstrated awareness of issues of own and client diversity. Please comment on how intern integrates awareness of diversity into therapeutic or assessment work.

IV. Capacity for autonomy. Please comment on how the intern demonstrates the capacity for autonomous functioning. Please note how or if s/he could benefit from additional support to develop this capacity.

V. Skills at oral and written communication. Please comment on the intern's capacity as a communicator in those modalities that you have observed. Please note any specific needs for editing observed in written communication, and how and whether the intern has responded to previous editing feedback.

VI. Ethics and boundaries. Please comment on the intern's demonstrated sensitivity to issues of ethics and boundaries for practice.

VII. Other. Please comment in detail as to other observations of this intern's capacities that you believe it would be useful for FCTP to know about. We are interested both in highly meritorious performance as well as performance that might, if unchanged, raise concerns.

Appendix B:
Sample Feminist
Supervision Agreement

LAURA S. BROWN, PHD, ABPP

Diplomate in Clinical Psychology

3429 Fremont Pl. North #319

Seattle, WA 98103

206-633-2405

laurabrownphd@gmail.com

SUPERVISION AGREEMENT

This constitutes an agreement between Laura S. Brown, PhD (supervisor) and _____ (resident) for the provision of supervision services by Dr. Brown to the resident. We agree to meet at on the schedule mutually decided upon, at a fee of $XX/session.

We agree to the following rights and responsibilities in this supervision relationship:

1. The supervisor and resident acknowledge that the supervisor has clinical and legal responsibility for the acts and omissions of the resident. As such, the resident agrees to abide by the supervisor's advice and

direction regarding possible risks in practice. The supervisor agrees to offer such advice and direction as needed to protect the welfare of the resident and her or his clients. Failure by the resident to inform the supervisor of risk, as described below, will be considered as an abrogation of this contract by the resident. The resident will inform the supervisor of potential risk situations by voicemail, cellphone, or email within 24 hours, and follow up on these issues at the next scheduled supervision meeting. The supervisor may be available between scheduled consultation sessions for additional consultation in person or by phone as needed on an emergent basis. When the supervisor is on vacation, the resident will arrange her or his own back-up supervision. Risk situations are defined as follows for purposes of this agreement:

- any client who is at imminent risk of harm to self or others,
- any client who reports suspected child or vulnerable adult abuse, or
- any client reporting erotic or violent feelings toward the resident therapist.

2. Resident will maintain her/his own professional liability insurance coverage at all times. Resident will not be covered by supervisor's liability insurance. Resident will maintain licensure or certification in jurisdiction of practice appropriate to her/his training. Resident agrees to abide by the most recent revision of the Ethics Code of the American Psychological Association or the appropriate professional association with which she or he is affiliated.

3. The content of supervision sessions will be held in confidence with the following exceptions: (a) If resident releases supervisor in writing to share information for specific purposes; (b) if supervisor receives a court order requiring release of information; (c) if resident persists in actions that supervisor has advised are ethically or legally potentially actionable. Supervisor reserves the right at this time to report resident to regulatory or ethical authorities, and to terminate supervision services if this should occur. Resident is free to terminate supervision services at any time, at which point supervisor will cease to hold legal and clinical responsibility for the clients treated by resident.

4. Resident will provide supervisor with copies of case notes on all clients under supervision on request. Case notes shall conform to standards for note-taking as defined by the resident's profession. Supervisor will complete, as needed, all forms attesting to the supervision of the resident that might be needed for resident's further credentialing.

5. Resident understands that the supervisor may request audiotaping of sessions and random review of audiotapes for purposes of resident education and/or quality control. The resident will inform all new clients in writing, in an office policy statement, of her or his residency status, the identity of the supervisor, and the potential for audiotaping for purposes of supervision.

6. Resident understands that the supervisor must report any impairment for any reason to the Dept. of Health, as mandated by Washington State Law.

Resident is free to terminate supervision services at any time.

I understand and agree to the terms of this supervision agreement.

Signed:_____Date:_____

      Resident

Signed:_____Date:_____

      Supervisor

Appendix C:
Sample Private Practice Consultation Agreement— Professional Consultation Services Agreement

This constitutes an agreement between Laura S. Brown, PhD (consultant) and _____(consultee) for the provision of consultation services by Dr. Brown to the consultee. We agree to meet at an interval to be mutually arranged. The fee for a consultation session, which will last 45 minutes, will be $XX. Fees will be raised $10.00 in even-numbered years. Extra time spent in consultation (e.g., between sessions on phone or email) will be charged at a prorated fee.

We agree to the following rights and responsibilities in this consultation relationship:

1. Notification of risk. The consultant may be available between scheduled consultation sessions for additional consultation in person or by phone as needed on an emergent basis. The consultee is not responsible for notifying consultant of risk.

2. Liability. Consultee will maintain her/his own professional liability insurance coverage at all times. Consultee will not be covered by

consultant's liability insurance. Consultant is not the employer or supervisor of the consultee, and is not responsible for any acts or omissions of the consultee. Consultee will maintain licensure or certification in state or province of practice appropriate to her/his training.

3. Confidentiality. The content of consultation sessions will be held in confidence with the following exceptions: (a) If consultee releases consultant in writing to share information for specific purposes; (b) if consultant receives a court order requiring release of information; (c) if consultee persists in actions that consultant has advised are ethically or legally potentially actionable (consultant reserves the right at this time to report consultee to regulatory or ethical authorities, and to terminate consultation services); (d) if consultant determines that consultee is an impaired practitioner, consultant must report consultee to her/his licensing authority per Washington State law on impaired practitioners.

Consultee is free to terminate consultation services at any time.

I understand and agree to the terms of this consultation agreement.

Appendix D:
Feminist Therapy Institute Code of Ethics (Revised, 1999)

Preamble

Feminist therapy evolved from feminist philosophy, psychological theory and practice, and political theory. In particular feminists recognize the impact of society in creating and maintaining the problems and issues brought into therapy.

Briefly, feminists believe the personal is political. Basic tenets of feminism include a belief in the equal worth of all human beings, a recognition that each individual's personal experiences and situations are reflective of and an influence on society's institutionalized attitudes and values, and a commitment to political and social change that equalizes power among people. Feminists are committed to recognizing and reducing the pervasive influences and insidious effects of oppressive societal attitudes and society.

Thus, a feminist analysis addresses the understanding of power and its interconnections among gender, race, culture, class, physical ability, sexual orientation, age, and anti-Semitism as well as all forms of oppression based on religion, ethnicity, and heritage. Feminist therapists also live in and are subject to those same influences and effects and consistently monitor their beliefs and behaviors as a result of those influences.

Feminist therapists adhere to and integrate feminist analyses in all spheres of their work as therapists, educators, consultants, administrators, writers, editors, and/or researchers. Feminist therapists are accountable for the management of the power differential within these roles and accept responsibility for that power. Because of the limitations of a purely intra-psychic model of human functioning, feminist therapists facilitate the understanding of the interactive effects of the client's internal and external worlds. Feminist therapists possess knowledge about the psychology of women and girls and utilize feminist scholarship to revise theories and practices, incorporating new knowledge as it is generated.

Feminist therapists are trained in a variety of disciplines, theoretical orientations, and degrees of structure. They come from different cultural, economic, ethnic, and racial backgrounds. They work in many types of settings with a diversity of clients and practice different modalities of therapy, training, and research. Feminist therapy theory integrates feminist principles into other theories of human development and change.

The ethical guidelines that follow are additive to, rather than a replacement for, the ethical principles of the profession in which a feminist therapist practices. Amid this diversity, feminist therapists are joined together by their feminist analyses and perspectives. Additionally, they work toward incorporating feminist principles into existing professional standards when appropriate.

Feminist therapists live with and practice in competing forces and complex controlling interests. When mental health care involves third-party payers, it is feminist therapists' responsibility to advocate for the best possible therapeutic process for the client, including short- or long-term therapy. Care and compassion for clients include protection of confidentiality and awareness of the impacts of economic and political considerations, including the increasing disparity between the quality of therapeutic care available for those with or without third-party payers.

Feminist therapists assume a proactive stance toward the eradication of oppression in their lives and work toward empowering women and girls. They are respectful of individual differences, examining oppressive aspects of both their own and clients' value systems. Feminist therapists engage in social change activities, broadly defined, outside of and apart from their work in their professions. Such activities may vary in scope and content but are an essential aspect of a feminist perspective.

This code is a series of positive statements that provide guidelines for feminist therapy practice, training, and research. Feminist therapists who are members of other professional organizations adhere to the ethical codes of those organizations. Feminist therapists who are not members of such organizations are guided by the ethical standards of the organization closest to their mode of practice.

These statements provide more specific guidelines within the context of and as an extension of most ethical codes. When ethical guidelines are in conflict, the feminist therapist is accountable for how she prioritizes her choices.

These ethical guidelines, then, are focused on the issues feminist therapists, educators, and researchers have found especially important in their professional settings. As with any code of therapy ethics, the well-being of clients is the guiding principle underlying this code. The feminist therapy issues that relate directly to the client's well being include cultural diversities and oppressions, power differentials, overlapping relationships, therapist accountability, and social change. Even though the principles are stated separately, each interfaces with the others to form an interdependent whole. In addition, the code is a living document and thus is continually in the process of change.

The Feminist Therapy Institute's Code of Ethics is shaped by economic and cultural forces in North America and by the experiences of its members. Members encourage an ongoing international dialogue about feminist and ethical issues. It recognizes that ethical codes are aspirational and ethical behaviors are on a continuum rather than reflecting dichotomies. Additionally, ethical guidelines and legal requirements may differ. The Feminist Therapy Institute provides educational interventions for its members rather than disciplinary activity.

Ethical Guidelines for Feminist Therapists

I. Cultural Diversities and Oppressions

A. A feminist therapist increases her accessibility to and for a wide range of clients from her own and other identified groups through flexible delivery of services. When appropriate, the feminist therapist assists clients in accessing other services and intervenes when a client's rights are violated.

B. A feminist therapist is aware of the meaning and impact of her own ethnic and cultural background, gender, class, age, and sexual orientation, and actively attempts to become knowledgeable about alternatives from sources other than her clients. She is actively engaged in broadening her knowledge of ethnic and cultural experiences, non-dominant and dominant.

C. Recognizing that the dominant culture determines the norm, the therapist's goal is to uncover and respect cultural and experiential differences, including those based on long term or recent immigration and/or refugee status.

D. A feminist therapist evaluates her ongoing interactions with her clientele for any evidence of her biases or discriminatory attitudes and practices. She also monitors her other interactions, including service delivery, teaching, writing, and all professional activities. The feminist therapist accepts responsibility for taking action to confront and change any interfering, oppressing, or devaluing biases she has.

II. Power Differentials

A. A feminist therapist acknowledges the inherent power differentials between client and therapist and models effective use of personal, structural, or institutional power. In using the power differential to the benefit of the client, she does not take control or power that rightfully belongs to her client.

B. A feminist therapist discloses information to the client that facilitates the therapeutic process, including information communicated to others. The therapist is responsible for using self-disclosure only with purpose and discretion and in the interest of the client.

C. A feminist therapist negotiates and renegotiates formal and/or informal contacts with clients in an ongoing mutual process. As part of the decision-making process, she makes explicit the therapeutic issues involved.

D. A feminist therapist educates her clients regarding power relationships. She informs clients of their rights as consumers of therapy, including procedures for resolving differences and filing grievances. She clarifies power in its various forms, as it exists within other areas of her life, including professional roles, social/governmental structures, and interpersonal relationships. She assists her clients in finding ways to protect themselves and, if requested, to seek redress.

III. Overlapping Relationships

A. A feminist therapist recognizes the complexity and conflicting priorities inherent in multiple or overlapping relationships. The therapist accepts responsibility for monitoring such relationships to prevent potential abuse of or harm to the client.

B. A feminist therapist is actively involved in her community. As a result, she is aware of the need for confidentiality in all settings. Recognizing that her client's concerns and general well-being are primary, she self-monitors both public and private statements and comments. Situations may develop through community involvement where power dynamics shift, including a client having equal or more authority than the therapist. In all such situations a feminist therapist maintains accountability.

C. When accepting third-party payments, a feminist therapist is especially cognizant of and clearly communicates to her client the multiple obligations, roles, and responsibilities of the therapist. When working in institutional settings, she clarifies to all involved parties where her allegiances lie. She also monitors multiple and conflicting expectations between clients and caregivers, especially when working with children and elders.

D. A feminist therapist does not engage in sexual intimacies nor any overtly or covertly sexualized behaviors with a client or former client.

IV. Therapist Accountability

A. A feminist therapist is accountable to herself, to colleagues, and especially to her clients.

B. A feminist therapist will contract to work with clients and issues within the realm of her competencies. If problems beyond her competencies surface, the feminist therapist utilizes consultation and available resources. She respects the integrity of the relationship by stating the limits of her training and providing the client with the possibilities of continuing with her or changing therapists.

C. A feminist therapist recognizes her personal and professional needs and utilizes ongoing self-evaluation, peer support, consultation, supervision, continuing education, and/or personal therapy. She evaluates, maintains, and seeks to improve her competencies, as well as her emotional, physical, mental, and spiritual well-being. When the feminist therapist has experienced a similar stressful or damaging event as her client, she seeks consultation.

D. A feminist therapist continually re-evaluates her training, theoretical background, and research to include developments in feminist knowledge. She integrates feminism into psychological theory, receives ongoing therapy training, and acknowledges the limits of her competencies.

E. A feminist therapist engages in self-care activities in an ongoing manner outside the work setting. She recognizes her own needs and vulnerabilities as well as the unique stresses inherent in this work. She demonstrates an ability to establish boundaries with the client that are healthy for both of them. She also is willing to self-nurture in appropriate and self-empowering ways.

V. Social Change

A. A feminist therapist seeks multiple avenues for impacting change, including public education and advocacy within professional organizations, lobbying for legislative actions, and other appropriate activities.

B. A feminist therapist actively questions practices in her community that appear harmful to clients or therapists. She assists clients in intervening on their own behalf. As appropriate, the feminist therapist herself intervenes, especially when other practitioners appear to be engaging in harmful, unethical, or illegal behaviors.

C. When appropriate, a feminist therapist encourages a client's recognition of criminal behaviors and also facilitates the client's navigation of the criminal justice system.

D. A feminist therapist, teacher, or researcher is alert to the control of information dissemination and questions pressures to conform to and use dominant mainstream standards. As technological methods of communication change and increase, the feminist therapist recognizes the socioeconomic aspects of these developments and communicates according to clients' access to technology.

E. A feminist therapist, teacher, or researcher recognizes the political is personal in a world where social change is a constant.

Suggested Readings

Ballou, M., & Brown, L. S. (Eds.). (2000). *Rethinking mental health and disorder: Feminist perspectives.* New York, NY: Guilford.

Ballou, M., Hill, M., & West, C. (Eds.). (2008). *Feminist theory and practice.* New York, NY: Springer Publishing.

Brown, L. S. (2010). *Feminist therapy.* Washington, DC: American Psychological Association.

Porter, N. (2009). Feminist and multicultural underpinnings to supervision: An overview. *Women & Therapy, 33,* 1–6. This is the introductory article of a special issue of the journal, the entirety of which is suggested reading.

Szymanski, D. (2003). The feminist supervision scale: A rational/theoretical approach. *Psychology of Women Quarterly, 27,* 221–232. This is the first of Szymanski's many and valuable articles on this topic. Feminist supervisors will benefit from doing a literature search to find her most current work, some of which can be found cited in the References section of this book.

References

Arczynski, A. V. (2014). *Multicultural psychotherapy supervision: A qualitative study* (Unpublished doctoral dissertation). Department of Educational Psychology, University of Utah, Salt Lake City.

Baird, M. K., Szymanski, D. M., & Ruebelt, S. G. (2007). Feminist identity development and practice among male therapists. *Psychology of Men & Masculinity, 8,* 67–78. http://dx.doi.org/10.1037/1524-9220.8.2.67

Baker Miller, J., & Welch, A. S. (1995). Learning from women. In P. Chesler, E. D. Rothblum, & E. Cole (Eds.), *Feminist foremothers in women's studies, psychology and mental health* (pp. 335–346). Binghamton, NY: Haworth Press.

Ballou, M., & Brown, L. (Eds.). (2000). *Rethinking mental health and disorder: Feminist perspectives.* New York, NY: Guilford.

Ballou, M., Hill, M., & West, C. (Eds.). (2008). *Feminist therapy theory and practice.* New York, NY: Springer.

Ballou, M., Matsumoto, A., & Wagner, M. (2002). Toward a feminist ecological theory of human nature: Theory building in response to real world dynamics. In M. Ballou & L. S. Brown (Eds.), *Rethinking mental health and disorder: Feminist perspectives* (pp. 99–144). New York, NY: Guilford.

Berman, J. S. (1985). Ethical feminist perspectives on dual relationships with clients. In L. B. Rosewater & L. E. A. Walker (Eds.), *Handbook of feminist therapy: Women's issues in psychotherapy* (pp. 286–296). New York, NY: Springer.

Bernardez, T. (1995). By my sisters reborn. In P. Chesler, E. D. Rothblum, & E. Cole (Eds.), *Feminist foremothers in women's studies, psychology and mental health* (pp. 55–70). Binghamton, NY: Haworth Press.

Broverman, I. K., Broverman, D. M., Clarkson, F. E., Rosenkrantz, P. S., & Vogel, S. R. (1970). Sex-role stereotypes and clinical judgments of mental health.

Journal of Consulting and Clinical Psychology, 34, 1–7. http://dx.doi.org/10.1037/h0028797

Brown, L. S. (1985). Power, responsibility, boundaries: Ethical issues for the lesbian-feminist therapist. *Lesbian Ethics, 1*, 30–45.

Brown, L. S. (1991). Ethical issues in feminist therapy: Selected topics. *Psychology of Women Quarterly, 15*, 323–336. http://dx.doi.org/10.1111/j.1471-6402.1991.tb00800.x

Brown, L. S. (1994). *Subversive dialogues: Theory in feminist therapy.* New York, NY: Basic Books.

Brown, L. S. (1995). Antiracism as an ethical norm in feminist therapy. In J. Adelman & G. Enguidanos (Eds.), *Racism in the lives of women* (pp. 137–148). Binghamton, NY: Haworth Press.

Brown, L. S. (1997). Ethics in psychology: Cui bono? In D. Fox & I. Prilleltensky (Eds.), *The handbook of critical psychology* (pp. 51–67). Thousand Oaks, CA: Sage Publications.

Brown, L. S. (2006). Still subversive after all these years: The relevance of feminist therapy in the age of evidence-based practice. *Psychology of Women Quarterly, 30*, 15–24. http://dx.doi.org/10.1111/j.1471-6402.2006.00258.x

Brown, L. S. (2007). Empathy, genuineness—and the dynamics of power: A feminist responds to Rogers. *Psychotherapy: Theory, Research, Practice, Training, 44*, 257–259.

Brown, L. S. (2008). *Cultural competence in trauma therapy: Beyond the flashback.* Washington, DC: American Psychological Association.

Brown, L. S. (2010). *Feminist therapy.* Washington, DC: American Psychological Association.

Brown, L. S. (2012a). On not quitting my day job. In M. Hoyt (Ed.), *Therapist stories of inspiration, passion and renewal: What's love got to do with it?* (pp. 36–45). New York, NY: Routledge.

Brown, L. S. (2012b). Compassion amidst oppression: Increasing cultural competence for managing difficult dialogues in therapy. In M. Goldfried, A. Wolf, & J. C. Muran (Eds.), *Transforming negative reactions to clients: From frustration to compassion* (pp. 139–158). Washington, DC: American Psychological Association.

Brown, L. S., & Ballou, M. (Eds.). (1992). *Personality and psychopathology: Feminist reappraisals.* New York, NY: Guilford Publications.

Brown, L. S., & Walker, L. E. A. (1990). Feminist therapy perspectives on self-disclosure. In G. Stricker & M. Fisher (Eds.), *Self-disclosure in the therapeutic relationship* (pp. 135–154). New York, NY: Plenum. http://dx.doi.org/10.1007/978-1-4899-3582-3_10

Bryan, T. C. (2012). *How the experience of being a survivor of complex trauma informs a therapist's work with trauma survivors: A crystallized and poetic inquiry into the wounded healer* (Unpublished doctoral dissertation). Washington School of Professional Psychology, Seattle, WA.

Caplan, P. (1995). Weak ego boundaries: One developing feminist's story. In P. Chesler, E. D. Rothblum, & E. Cole (Eds.), *Feminist foremothers in women's studies, psychology and mental health* (pp. 113–124). Binghamton, NY: Haworth Press.

Chandler, R., Worell, J., Johnson, D., Blount, A., & Lusk, M. (1999, August). Measuring long-term outcomes of feminist counseling and psychotherapy. In J. Worell (Chair), *Measuring process and outcomes in short-and long-term feminist therapy.* Symposium presented at the annual meeting of the American Psychological Association, Boston, MA.

Chesler, P. (1970). Patient and patriarch. In V. Gornick & B. K. Moran (Eds.), *Woman in sexist society: Studies in power and powerlessness* (pp. 362–392). New York, NY: Signet.

Chesler, P. (1972). *Women and madness.* Garden City, NY: Doubleday.

Chew, J. (in press). Feminist supervision: A model for knowledge and practice. In B. Shepard, B. Robinson, & L. Martin (Eds.), *Clinical supervision of the Canadian counselling and psychotherapy profession.* Ottawa, ON, Canada: CCPA.

Cole, E., Rothblum, E. D., & Chesler, P. (Eds.). (1995). *Feminist foremothers in women's studies, psychology, and mental health.* Binghamton, NY: Haworth Press.

Cole, K. L., Sarlund-Heinrich, P., & Brown, L. (2007). Developing and assessing effectiveness of a time-limited therapy group for incarcerated women survivors of childhood sexual abuse. *Journal of Trauma & Dissociation, 8,* 97–121. http://dx.doi.org/10.1300/J229v08n02_07

Comas-Díaz, L. (2012). *Multicultural care: A clinician's guide to cultural competence.* Washington, DC: American Psychological Association. http://dx.doi.org/10.1037/13491-000

Comas-Díaz, L., & Greene, B. A. (Eds.). (2013). *Psychological health of women of color.* New York, NY: Guilford.

Denmark, F. (1995). Feminist and activist. In P. Chesler, E. D. Rothblum, & E. Cole (Eds.), *Feminist foremothers in women's studies, psychology and mental health* (pp. 163–170). Binghamton, NY: Haworth Press.

Dovidio, J. F., Gaertner, S. L., Kawakami, K., & Hodson, G. (2002). Why can't we just get along? Interpersonal biases and interracial distrust. *Cultural Diversity and Ethnic Minority Psychology, 8,* 88–102.

Duncan, B., Miller, C., & Wampold, B. (Eds.). (2009). *The heart and soul of change.* Washington, DC: American Psychological Association.

Dutton, M. A., & Rave, E. J. (1990). Ethics of feminist supervision of psychotherapy. In H. Lerman & N. Porter (Eds.), *Feminist ethics in psychotherapy* (pp. 137–146). New York, NY: Springer.

Englar-Carlson, M., & Stevens, M. (Eds.). (2006). *In the room with men: A casebook of therapeutic change.* Washington, DC: American Psychological Association.

Enns, C. Z. (1992). Toward integrating feminist psychotherapy and feminist philosophy. *Professional Psychology: Research and Practice, 23,* 453–466. http://dx.doi.org/10.1037/0735-7028.23.6.453

Enns, C. Z. (2004). *Feminist theories and feminist psychotherapies: Origins, themes and variations.* Binghamton, NY: Haworth Press.

Enns, C. Z., & Forrest, L. (2005). Toward defining and integrating multicultural and feminist pedagogies. In C. Z. Enns & A. L. Sinacore (Eds.), *Teaching and social justice: Integrating multicultural and feminist theories in the classroom* (pp. 3–23). Washington, DC: American Psychological Association. http://dx.doi.org/10.1037/10929-001

Enns, C. Z., & Sinacore, A. L. (Eds.). (2005). *Teaching and social justice: Integrating multicultural and feminist theories in the classroom.* Washington, DC: American Psychological Association.

Enns, C. Z., Williams, E. N., & Fassinger, R. E. (2013). Feminist multicultural psychology: Change and challenge. In C. Z. Enns & E. N. Williams (Eds.), *The Oxford handbook of feminist multicultural psychology* (pp. 3–26). New York, NY: Oxford University Press.

Falender, C. (2010). Relationship and accountability: Tensions in feminist supervision. *Women & Therapy, 33,* 22–41.

Faunce, P. S. (1985). A feminist philosophy of treatment. In L. B. Rosewater & L. E. A. Walker, (Eds.), *Handbook of feminist therapy: Women's issues in psychotherapy* (pp. 1–5). New York, NY: Springer.

Feminist Therapy Institute. (1990). Feminist Therapy Institute code of ethics. In H. Lerman & N. Porter (Eds.), *Feminist ethics in psychotherapy* (pp. 37–40). New York, NY: Springer.

Feminist Therapy Institute. (1995). Feminist Therapy Institute code of ethics (Revised). In E. J. Rave & C. C. Larsen (Eds.), *Ethical decision-making in therapy: Feminist perspectives* (pp. 38–41). New York, NY: Guilford.

Feminist Therapy Institute. (1999). *Feminist Therapy Institute code of ethics.* Denver, CO: Author.

Fischer, A. R., Tokar, D. M., Mergl, M. M., Good, G. E., Hill, M. S., & Blum, S. A. (2000). Assessing women's feminist identity development: Studies of convergent, discriminate, and structural validity. *Psychology of Women Quarterly, 24,* 15–29. http://dx.doi.org/10.1111/j.1471-6402.2000.tb01018.x

Fisher, B. M. (1981). What is feminist pedagogy? *Radical Teacher, 18,* 20–24.

Freire, P. (1968). *Pedagogy of the oppressed.* New York, NY: Continuum.

Gartrell, N. (1995). Lesbian feminist fights organized psychiatry. In P. Chesler, E. D. Rothblum, & E. Cole (Eds.), *Feminist foremothers in women's studies, psychology and mental health* (pp. 205–212). Binghamton, NY: Haworth Press.

Gentile, L., Ballou, M., Roffman, E., & Ritchie, J. (2009). Supervision for social change: A feminist ecological perspective. *Women & Therapy, 33,* 140–151. http://dx.doi.org/10.1080/02703140903404929

Giddings, P. (1996). *When and where I enter: The impact of race and sex on Black women's lives.* New York, NY: Amistad.

Goodman, L., Liang, B., Helms, J., Latta, R., Sparks, E., & Weintraub, S. (2004). Training counseling psychologists as social justice agents: Feminist and multicultural principles in action. *The Counseling Psychologist, 32,* 793–836. http://dx.doi.org/10.1177/0011000004268802

Green, M. S., & Dekkers, T. D. (2010). Attending to power and diversity in supervision: An exploration of supervisee learning outcomes and satisfaction with supervision. *Journal of Feminist Family Therapy, 22*(4), 293–312. http://dx.doi.org/10.1080/08952833.2010.528703

Greenspan, M. (1982). *A new approach to women and therapy.* New York, NY: McGraw Hill.

Greenspan, M. (1995). On being a feminist and a psychotherapist. In P. Chesler, E. D. Rothblum, & E. Cole (Eds.), *Feminist foremothers in women's studies, psychology and mental health* (pp. 229–242). Binghamton, NY: Haworth Press.

Hare-Mustin, R. T., Marecek, J., Kaplan, A. G., & Liss-Levinson, N. (1979). Rights of clients, responsibilities of therapists. *American Psychologist, 34,* 3–16. http://dx.doi.org/10.1037/0003-066X.34.1.3

Hays, P. A. (2008). *Addressing cultural complexities in practice: Assessment, diagnosis, and therapy* (2nd ed.). Washington, DC: American Psychological Association. http://dx.doi.org/10.1037/11650-000

Hill, C., & Knox, S. (2002). Self-disclosure. In J. C. Norcross, (Ed.), *Psychotherapy relationships that work: Therapist contributions and responsiveness to patients* (pp. 255–266). New York, NY: Oxford University Press.

Hyde, J. S. (2005). The gender similarities hypothesis. *American Psychologist, 60,* 581–592.

Kanuha, V. K. (1990). An integrated analysis of oppression in feminist therapy. In H. Lerman & N. Porter (Eds.), *Feminist ethics in psychotherapy* (pp. 24–36). New York, NY: Springer Publishing Company.

Kaschak, E. (1992). *Engendered lives.* New York, NY: Basic Books.

Lerman, H. (1983, May). *Criteria for a theory of feminist therapy.* Paper presented at the Second Advanced Feminist Therapy Institute, Washington, DC.

Lerman, H. (1996). *Pigeonholing women's misery.* New York, NY: Basic Books.

Lerman, H., & Porter, N. (Eds.). (1990). *Feminist ethics in psychotherapy.* New York, NY: Springer Publishing.

Lerner, G. (1993). *The creation of feminist consciousness.* New York, NY: Oxford University Press.

Luepnitz, D. A. (1988). *The family interpreted.* New York, NY: Basic Books.

MacKinnon, C. J., Bhatia, M., Sunderani, S., Affleck, W. A., & Smith, N. G. (2011). Opening the dialogue: Implications of feminist supervision theory with male supervisees. *Professional Psychology: Research and Practice, 42,* 130–136. http://dx.doi.org/10.1037/a0022232

Mangione, L., Mears, G., Vincent, W., & Hawes, S. (2011). The supervisory relationship when women supervise women: An exploratory study of power, reflexivity, collaboration, and authenticity. *The Clinical Supervisor, 30,* 141–171. http://dx.doi.org/10.1080/07325223.2011.604272

McIntosh, P. (1998). White privilege: Unpacking the invisible knapsack. In M. McGoldrick (Ed.), *Re-visioning family therapy: Race, culture and gender in clinical practice* (pp. 147–152). New York, NY: Guilford Press.

Mio, J. S., & Roades, L. A. (2003). Building bridges in the 21st century: Allies and the power of human connection across demographic divides. In J. S. Mio & G. Y. Iwamasa (Eds.), *Culturally diverse mental health: The challenges of research and resistance* (pp. 105–117). New York, NY: Brunner-Routledge.

Miville, M. (2013). Multicultural feminist training, supervision and continuing education: Concepts, competencies, and challenges. In C. Z. Enns & E. N. Williams (Eds.), *The Oxford handbook of feminist multicultural counseling psychology* (pp. 432–450). New York, NY: Oxford University Press.

Nelson, M. L., Gizara, S., Hope, A. C., Phelps, R., Steward, R., & Weitzman, L. (2006). A feminist multicultural perspective on supervision. *Journal of Multicultural Counseling and Development, 34,* 105–115. http://dx.doi.org/10.1002/j.2161-1912.2006.tb00031.x

Norcross, J. C. (2004). Tailoring the therapy relationship to the individual patient: Evidence-based practices. Invited distinguished contribution. *Clinician's Research Digest, Supplemental Bulletin, 30,* 1–2.

Norcross, J. C. (Ed.). (2011). *Psychotherapy relationships that work: Evidence-based responsiveness* (2nd ed.). New York, NY: Oxford University Press. http://dx.doi.org/10.1093/acprof:oso/9780199737208.001.0001

Oakley, M. A., Addison, S. C., Piran, N., Johnston, G. J., Damianakis, M., Curry, J., . . . Weigeldt, A. (2013). Outcome study of brief relational-cultural therapy in a women's mental health center. *Psychotherapy Research, 23,* 137–151. http://dx.doi.org/10.1080/10503307.2012.745956

Pape, K. M. (2010, February). "You need it, I can share it": Cooperation and growth in a feminist therapy training clinic. In L. S. Brown (Chair), *Creat-*

ing a feminist therapy community training clinic: Our experiences building the Fremont Community Therapy Project. Panel presented at the 35th Annual Conference of the Association for Women in Psychology, Portland, OR.

Payton, C. R. (1994). Implications of the 1992 ethics code for diverse groups. *Professional Psychology: Research and Practice, 25,* 317–320. http://dx.doi.org/10.1037/0735-7028.25.4.317

Pearlman, L. A., & Saakvitne, K. W. (1995). *Trauma and the therapist: Countertransference and vicarious traumatization in psychotherapy with incest survivors.* New York, NY: W. W. Norton.

Peterson, M. (1992). *At personal risk. Boundary violations in professional-client relationships.* New York, NY: W. W. Norton

Piran, N. (1999, August). The Feminist Frame Scale. In J. Worell (Chair), *Measuring process and outcomes in short- and long-term feminist therapy.* Symposium presented at the annual meeting of the American Psychological Association, Boston, MA.

Pope, K. S., & Feldman-Summers, S. (1992). National survey of psychologists' sexual and physical abuse history and their evaluation of training and competence in these areas. *Professional Psychology: Research and Practice, 23,* 353–361. http://dx.doi.org/10.1037/0735-7028.23.5.353

Pope, K. S., & Tabachnick, B. G. (1993). Therapists' anger, hate, fear, and sexual feelings: National survey of therapist responses, client characteristics, critical events, formal complaints, and training. *Professional Psychology: Research and Practice, 24,* 142–152. http://dx.doi.org/10.1037/0735-7028.24.2.142

Porter, N. (1985). New perspectives on therapy supervision. In L. B. Rosewater & L. E. A. Walker (Eds.), *Handbook of feminist therapy: Women's issues in psychotherapy* (pp. 332–343). New York, NY: Springer Publishing.

Porter, N. (2009). Feminist and multicultural underpinnings to supervision: An overview. *Women & Therapy, 33,* 1–6. http://dx.doi.org/10.1080/02703140903404622

Porter, N., & Vasquez, M. (1997). Covision: Feminist supervision, process, and collaboration. In J. Worell & N. Johnson (Eds.), *Shaping the future of feminist psychology: Education, research, and practice* (pp. 155–171). Washington, DC: American Psychological Association. http://dx.doi.org/10.1037/10245-007

Prouty, A. M. (2001). Experiencing feminist family therapy supervision. *Journal of Feminist Family Therapy, 12,* 171–203. http://dx.doi.org/10.1300/J086v12n04_01

Prouty, A. M., Thomas, V., Johnson, S., & Long, J. K. (2001). Methods of feminist family therapy supervision. *Journal of Marital and Family Therapy, 27,* 85–97. http://dx.doi.org/10.1111/j.1752-0606.2001.tb01141.x

Quina, K., & Brown, L. S. (Eds.) (2007). *Trauma and dissociation in convicted offenders.* Binghamton, NY: Haworth Medical Press.

Rader, J., & Gilbert, L. A. (2005). The egalitarian relationship in feminist therapy. *Psychology of Women Quarterly, 29,* 427–435.

Rawlings, E. I., & Carter, D. K. (1977). *Psychotherapy for women: Treatment towards equality.* Springfield, IL: Charles C. Thomas Publishers Ltd.

Rogers, C. R. (1957). The necessary and sufficient conditions of therapeutic personality change. *Journal of Consulting Psychology, 21,* 95–103.

Root, M. P. P. (1998). Experiences and processes affecting racial identity development: Preliminary results from the Biracial Sibling Project. *Cultural Diversity and Mental Health, 4,* 237–247. http://dx.doi.org/10.1037/1099-9809.4.3.237

Root, M. P. P. (2000). Rethinking racial identity development: An ecological framework. In P. Spickard & J. Burroughs (Eds.), *We are a people: Narrative in the construction and deconstruction of ethnic identity* (pp. 205–220). Philadelphia, PA: Temple University Press.

Rosewater, L. B., & Walker, L. E. A. (Eds.). (1985). *Handbook of feminist therapy: Women's issues in psychotherapy.* New York, NY: Springer Publishing.

Smith, A. J., & Siegel, R. F. (1985). Feminist therapy: Redefining power for the powerless. In L. B. Rosewater & L. E. A. Walker (Eds.), *Handbook of feminist therapy: Women's issues in psychotherapy* (pp. 13–21). New York, NY: Springer Publishing.

Swing, S. (2007, January). Why I'm a feminist. In D. Kawahara (Chair), *Voices of feminism and feminist therapy,* Panel Presentation, Fourth National Multicultural Conference and Summit, Seattle, WA.

Szymanski, D. (2003). The feminist supervision scale: A rational/theoretical approach. *Psychology of Women Quarterly, 27,* 221–232. http://dx.doi.org/10.1111/1471-6402.00102

Szymanski, D. (2005). Feminist identity and theories as correlates of feminist supervision practices. *The Counseling Psychologist, 33,* 729–747. http://dx.doi.org/10.1177/0011000005278408

Szymanski, D. M., Baird, M. K., & Kornman, C. L. (2002). The feminist male therapist: Attitudes and practices for the 21st century. *Psychology of Men & Masculinity, 3,* 22–27. http://dx.doi.org/10.1037/1524-9220.3.1.22

Unger, R. K. (1989). *Representations: Social constructions of gender.* Amityville, NY: Baywood Publishing.

Weisstein, N. (1968). *Kinder, kuche, kirche as scientific law: Psychology constructs the female.* Boston, MA: New England Free Press.

Worell, J., & Johnson, N. (Eds.). (1997). *Shaping the future of feminist psychology: Education, research, and practice.* Washington, DC: American Psychological Association.

Worell, J., & Remer, P. (2003). *Feminist perspectives in therapy: Empowering diverse women* (2nd ed.). Hoboken, NJ: John Wiley & Sons, Inc.

Index

About the Author

Laura S. Brown, PhD, ABPP, has been a practitioner of feminist psychotherapy, supervision, and forensic psychology since the 1970s. As the author of the foundational text *Subversive Dialogues: Theory in Feminist Therapy*, in addition to 11 other books and more than 150 articles and book chapters, she has been a major contributor to theory and practice in the fields of feminist psychotherapy and trauma treatment. Dr. Brown has been featured in several American Psychological Association (APA) DVDs about feminist therapy, trauma treatment, and feminist approaches to supervision, and has also lectured on these and related topics in the United States, Canada, Israel, Taiwan, Australia, and Europe. From 2006 to 2015, she directed the Fremont Community Therapy Project, a feminist therapy training clinic that she founded. She is a fellow of nine APA divisions, the Association for Psychological Science, and the International Society for the Study of Trauma and Dissociation. A late-in-life student of aikido, Dr. Brown was working toward her black belt at the time of this book's publication.